The Lit

MW01516539

Harold

Cruising Experiences on the West Coast

Les Bullis

Copyright © 2014 Les Bullis

All rights reserved.

ISBN:1499796846
ISBN-13:978=1499796841

For my children David and Nancy
Both of whom are boaters

Self Published

Printed by CreateSpace.com

Written by Les Bullis

Copies of this book available from
Amazon.com
Or from Author at
lesbullis@shaw.ca

CONTENTS

Foreward

At the time of writing this book I am in my late 70's and I thought it would be fun to jot down some of the mishaps that I experienced throughout my years of boating. All the stories are true and the experiences represent 60 plus years of boating in the Pacific Northwest. I'm sure all boaters can relate to these experiences because at one time or the other we've all been there. In my 60 plus years of boating most of my cruising time was spent trouble free. I have seen a lot of beautiful cruising areas and will treasure the memories forever. I have also been asked many times why my wife Dorothy and I live on the West Coast with all the rain and my stock answer is "if you were a boater you would understand".

I would like to thank the people whose names and boat names were used in this book. In particular, I would like to say thank you to the Haines family for being our boating companions for all these years.

Chapter One:

In The Beginning

I was born in Southern Oregon and was raised in a boating family. My parents tell me that I was less than two years old when they would bundle me up and put me under the bow of the boat while they were fishing on some of the local lakes. I was five or six when I first learned to row a boat. My uncle had a cabin on a lake in southern Oregon and the family would spend weekends at this cabin. They had a wooden boat that was about twelve or thirteen feet long and my older cousins would take me out on the lake and teach me how to row.

In the late 1940s we moved from southern Oregon to a small town on the Columbia River, a few miles north of Portland. After moving there my parents decided to buy a bigger boat that could be used to cruise up and down the Columbia. It was a 23 foot carvel planked cabin cruiser with an old Willies Jeep engine that had been converted for marine use. I can remember this engine was sitting in the middle of the cabin enclosed in a box and the top formed our eating table. The exhaust was a dry stack system. It came straight from the manifold into a muffler and up through the cabin roof. Without a water cooling system through the muffler it was very hot and if you came close to it you could get burned. The engine also had a unique fuel system: it didn't have a fuel pump so the gas tank was mounted forward under the bow with a gravity feed system down to the carburetor. We called this boat the *B-Liner.* It was with this boat that I remember our first unfortunate incident.

One time we had the boat out of the water on the weighs to do some remodeling work on the cabin interior. This required removing the helm station from the port side of the cabin to the starboard side. In those days the steering system of most boats was a cable wrapped around a drum attached to the steering wheel with the cable going down each side of the boat to the rudder. When the remodeling job was finished and the boat was ready to be put back into the water, we came off the weighs, back into the water and pushed the bow out toward the river. My father then gave the engine about half throttle and turned the wheel hard to port. The boat jumped ahead but turned hard to the starboard instead of port and ran about 20 feet dead center into a piling. There was a loud crunch and we were all thrown forward. We then had the boat pulled back out of the water to check for any damage and, of course, to rewind the steering cable the correct way. After finding no damage to the hull and, with the steering now operating properly, we put the boat back into the water.

In the 1950s I spent most of my spare time playing on the river and was known as one of the local river rats. When I was fourteen years old my father gave me my first boat. It was fourteen feet long with a four and one half foot beam. He built this boat from a kit back in the early 1940s. It was constructed of canvas over aluminum frames and was very light and easy to handle. By now my parents had sold the 23 foot cabin cruiser and bought a 1949 26 foot Chris-Craft in partnership with Dad's brother-in-law. The Chris-Craft was named the *B-Free* derived from the two family names "B" from Bullis and Free from Freeman. It was kept in a boat house moored at the local marina. My little lightweight boat was kept leaning on the outside of their boat house. That gave me easy access to it any time I wanted. My fellow river rats and I would row it down the river a few miles until a tug boat came along pulling a raft of logs up river. We would then row ourselves into the back wash of the log boom and sit there until we were pulled back up to our starting point. One winter I went down to the marina to check on the boat and it wasn't there. No one knew whether it had been stolen or was blown off the boat house during one of the winter storms but I never did see that boat again.

Every year our family would run the Chris Craft down the river and rent temporary moorage in Warrington, Oregon for the month of August to go salmon fishing on the mouth of the Columbia River. The salmon run always came from the ocean across the bar and followed the Washington shore as they made their way up stream. Being moored on the Oregon side meant that to get to the fishing grounds we had to cross the river. The mouth of the Columbia River is littered with sand bars and there were really only two ways to get from one side to the other: there was a marked channel that ran across about two miles inside the bar. Then there was another crossing about five miles up stream where the ferry went across. This was before the bridge was built.

When the tide begins to ebb and the wind starts blowing up stream the mouth of the Columbia can become quite rough in a very short period of time. One time we were fishing just inside the bar on the Washington side.

My favorite place to ride when we were underway was lying on the upper bunk just behind the helm station. I would wrap my feet around the rear strap that held the bunk up and hold onto the front strap for support. This way I could keep from being thrown off the bunk in rough seas.

It was getting late and we knew the tide was about to change to an ebb so we reeled in our lines and headed across to the Oregon side. Because it was late in the day and we were already near the lower crossing, we made the mistake of deciding to cross by the lower channel rather that take the time to travel the five miles upstream and cross at the safer ferry crossing.

We were about half way across and the seas were starting to get pretty rough and coming at us from the starboard side. Suddenly we were hit by a very large rogue wave that broke right over us. The boat took a roll to the port side and all I could see out the windows was green water. I was thrown off my bunk onto the floor. I thought for sure that we were going under so I jumped up and ran for the rear cabin door to get outside and keep from drowning. I had taken about two steps toward the rear of the boat when my dad's fishing partner grabbed me by the shirt and told me to look out back before I opened the door. I looked through the window and saw the back deck was covered with about four or five inches of water. Within a short time the water ran out the scuppers, which are holes cut into the side of the hull at deck level to let the water out, and the deck was high and dry again.

If I had opened the door earlier I would have let all that water come inside the boat and could have drowned out the engine. We made it across that day without any more trouble but I was sure one scared little boy!

49 Chris-Craft

One year we were running the boat back up river to bring it home. It was a nice warm day and one of my friends and I were lying on our backs on the back deck while my parents were inside the cabin running the boat. Boys being boys we had both brought along our home made sling shots and had gathered a pocket full of small round pebbles from the beach. We were shooting pebbles into the air and watching them fall in the water behind the boat.

We then got the idea to try and shoot the pebbles far enough ahead of the boat to see if we could get them to land onto the back deck where we were lying. I shot one into the air and suddenly there was this loud crash. The two front windows of this boat swung open from the bottom to allow for ventilation through the cabin. It was a hot day and both of these windows were open. My pebble came down and shattered the glass in the window opposite the helm station. At first my parents thought that they had been hit by a bullet from someone shooting a gun from shore. I thought about letting them think that was the case but then decided it was best to confess what I had done. I received a scolding but was also praised for telling the truth.

After losing the canvas boat, I started saving my paper route money and worked odd jobs until I had enough money to buy a factory built outboard powered boat. It was constructed of plywood over fir frames, was fourteen feet long and had a larger beam. This boat was built by the Storm King Boat Builders in Oregon and had a big five horsepower Johnson outboard motor. It also came with a factory built trailer. I named this boat *The* M*ermaid.*

It was with this boat that my adventures and mis-adventures really began. I remember one time when I was about sixteen years old a friend of mine owned a 1937 Ford sedan. We decided that it would be great if we took his car and my boat to go camping and fishing on a lake in eastern Oregon. We needed to get permission from our parents first and that took a lot of convincing! My father was concerned about the fact that a 1937 Ford had mechanical brakes and these were not as reliable as the new modern day hydraulic brakes. Pulling a boat with that car was not the best idea.

Somehow we managed to convince our folks we had checked the brake mechanism and that it was in good working order and we would be very careful. After a very long discussion they finally allowed us to make the trip.

One problem was not mentioned to our parents. The car did not have a trailer hitch. Not to worry, there is a solution to every problem. Our solution was to buy one of those "clamp on the bumper" type hitches. We gathered together all our camping gear and two other friends. With gear stored in the boat and four young men in a car with unreliable breaks and a trailer hitch clamped to a rather flimsy bumper we headed out to go camping and fishing. Everything went well and we made it to the lake without any problems. After a very enjoyable weekend of camping and fishing (and without much sleep) we packed up our gear, hooked up the boat and four tired guys headed for home.

As it turned out it was not the mechanical brakes that caused our trouble but the clamp on trailer hitch. We were traveling along this narrow and twisty two lane highway when John, the owner and driver of the car, looked out his side view mirror and said "Hey guys, what should we do about this boat that is about to pass us?" I was in the back seat and quickly turned around just in time to see the boat running right next to me. About that time the safety chain (yes, we were smart enough to have hooked up one) took hold and pulled the boat and trailer into the side of the car. John slowly let up on the throttle and gently applied the brakes. He managed to bring the whole thing to a slow halt alongside the road without having a serious accident.

We all got out and looked to see what had happened. Here was my boat trailer sitting with the front on the ground and the hitch still attached to the trailer. We simply bolted the hitch back onto the bumper and headed on home, this time stopping periodically to check that all was still secure. The car received a small dent in the rear fender and there was no damage to the boat. There was no mention of the incident to our parents.

Another time a bunch of us river rats were out on the water when one of my friends had left his boat on the beach and the tide went out leaving it high and dry. I decided that if I took a long rope and with my boat and trusty five horsepower outboard motor I could pull him off the beach. In theory it should have worked, but the rope we had was not quite long enough to allow me to get my boat out into deep water. I was in only about three feet of water and by running the outboard in that shallow water I didn't realize that I was sucking a lot of sand through the cooling system. It wasn't long before my motor seized from over heating. The sand had worn down the water pump impeller to where it wasn't pumping any cooling water through the engine.

After rowing my boat back to the marina, I took the motor to the repair shop to see about getting it running again. I was told that the motor was ruined beyond repair. Now I had to start saving for another outboard motor.

My next boat was a sixteen-foot plywood Birchcraft. While looking for a motor to replace the one I had ruined I came across the Birchcraft. It came with a large seven horsepower Evinrude outboard motor complete with forward and reverse shifting. I had a chance to sell the Storm King so I took the offer and bought the Birchcraft. I kept the trailer from the old boat and with a little alteration the Birchcraft fit very nicely.

I spent a few summers with my parents fishing the mouth of the Columbia and gathered a lot of experience and respect for the Columbia River bar. Subsequently I was allowed to take my own boat and go fishing at the mouth of the Columbia River. By this time I had my own car and I would usually take a friend with me and we would tow the boat and trailer down river. We set up our tent and camped in a campsite just up river from the little town of Chinook, Washington, and usually stayed for about a week. The boat could be launched from the beach just across the road from our campsite and we would keep it there above high tide at night.

I had very strict orders to fish only in the river and not to go below the mouth of Ilwaco Channel. I was told to watch the tides very closely and not to get caught near the mouth on an outgoing tide. I tried to adhere to this policy but as it turned out I could still get into trouble. One beautiful calm day my fishing partner and I were having great luck catching salmon. It was high slack tide and about to turn to an outgoing tide. We were just getting ready to pull in our lines and head up river when

I hooked a nice big salmon. It took almost one half hour to get this fish into the boat. Without our realizing it, the tide had started to run out and we had drifted below the Ilwaco Channel and almost to the North Jetty. We quickly started the motor and headed up stream.

By this time the wind had come up and the sea was getting rough. My little seven horsepower motor on a sixteen foot boat with two people in it would just get the boat up on a plane. We were making a little headway, but as time went by the current got stronger. We still had quite a way to go to the Ilwaco Channel. By taking a fix on a dolphin off shore, we discovered that we were moving backwards. There was a sandy beach near by. We decided it was best if we tried to run the boat up onto the beach and wait for the tide to change. By this time the sea conditions were getting very bad and there were breakers rolling onto the shore. I don't know why, but I decided that it would be best to bring the boat onto the beach with the bow out against the breakers. As we got close to shore I was just turning to put the bow out when my friend in the bow yelled "Look out!" I turned my head in time to see this large wave coming at us. The wave hit us broadside. The boat was tipped on its side as it hit the beach and both of us along with all our gear, including the freshly caught fish, were thrown into the surf. I cut my finger on the motor trying to keep it on the boat but that was the only injury suffered.

We pulled the boat further onto the beach and spent the next one half hour bailing water out of the boat and picking up fish and fishing gear off the beach. We sat there for almost four hours until the tide turned and we could head for camp. It was now getting dark and we were cold and wet. We made our way back to camp. We started a fire and warmed ourselves up and dried our clothes. This was a lesson well learned.

On another occasion, I took the boat down and camped near Chinook. A friend and I had gone fishing in the morning and by around noon we hadn't even had a bite. We decided that it was such a nice warm August Saturday, why not quit fishing and take my 1946 Chevrolet convertible across the ferry to Oregon and spend the rest of the day in Seaside, Oregon. This was before a bridge had been built across from Astoria.

Seaside is an ocean resort town about fifteen miles south of Astoria where a lot of the young people would converge on weekends to meet friends.

We arrived in Seaside in the late afternoon and immediately ran into some friends from home. We were all having a great time cruising up and down the main street in my convertible, top down, whistling at the girls. Then one of the guys asked, "Where are you guys going to stay tonight?"

I said, "Back at our camp in Chinook, why do you ask"?

"What time does the last ferry go across"? he asked.

I said "I think at eleven-thirty".

He looked at his watch and said "You're going to have to hurry, it's already eleven o clock".

We dropped our friends off and rushed to catch the last ferry from Astoria. I was pushing the car pretty hard and I'm sure we were breaking the speed limit. We were the last car to get onto the ferry and as we were driving on I could hear this knocking noise coming from the engine. I thought the noise was a worn rod bearing so the next morning I decided to take the car into a service garage in Chinook to get a professional opinion. The mechanic confirmed that it was a loose rod bearing and asked when I had last checked my engine oil? I had been too busy having fun to think about engine oil!

I explained to the man that I had to pull a boat and all my camping gear about 50 miles to get home. He said by the sound of it he didn't think I would make it. He put the car up on the hoist and looked things over. He thought he could probably drop the pan far enough to get to the rod and install a new bearing. He then gave me an estimate on the repairs. This turned out to be much more money than what I had on me. Regretfully, I had no alternative but to call my father for advice. He said that he would drive down the next day and we would then decide what to do. As it turned out, we had the garage install a new rod bearing and I made it home without any trouble. I then had to take money from my savings to repay my father.

I drove that car for another year and a half before selling it and never did lose that rod bearing. But I always made sure that the engine oil didn't get low again.

When Dorothy and I were first married, I still owned the sixteen-foot Birchcraft boat with the seven horsepower outboard motor. In the mid 1950s Johnson Motors introduced a 25 horsepower outboard motor. This new motor had enough power to pull water-skiers. However, boaters that had smaller motors couldn't pull a water-skier, so we would surfboard.

A surfboard back then was a flat board about three feet wide and four feet long, with a rounded front. There was a rope attached to the front that looped from one side to the other for the rider to hold on to. The rope that pulled the board was attached to the bottom of the board near the front. The rider would start off on his knees. As the board gained momentum, carefully keeping his balance, he'd come to a standing position. I built a surfboard from plywood and Dorothy and I surfed often.

When we took our friends, Don and Lavenia Wilson boating, Don wanted to learn how to surfboard. We put Don on the board and instructed him on how to surf. After falling a few times, Don found his balance and was doing well. Then I felt a heavy drag on the boat. Suddenly there was no pull against the boat at all. Lavenia yelled. I looked back to find that Don was nowhere in sight. We saw him surface, shaking his head and spitting water. I turned the boat around and went back to pick him up. When we came alongside Don, Lavenia asked, "What happened?"

Don said, "Your surfboard is on the bottom stuck under a log. If you want it back you can go after it yourself."

He then realized he'd lost his swimsuit! We threw him a towel and helped him aboard. We discovered Don had moved too far forward on the board, and that caused the front of the board to go underwater. He'd ridden it clear to the bottom! Luckily, we were in less than twenty feet of water. Don never did get on a surfboard again.

I later sold the seven horsepower motor and bought a used thirty-three horsepower Scott Attwater outboard motor. Soon after buying the larger motor, Dorothy and I decided to try it out on the water. We phoned a friend and invited him to come along. At this time Dorothy was eight months pregnant. We thought that rather than run out onto the Columbia River where the water could get rough, we'd take a run up one of the little sloughs that branched off the river. We motored up the slough a little over a mile and then started back.

Suddenly, the motor stopped. We were surprised to discover we had run out of fuel as we were unaware of how much fuel the larger motor used. We tied our boat to a log raft, hoping that someone would come by and rescue us. We waited for over an hour and saw no one.

We figured we were less than a half mile from the marina if we were to go overland. One of the guys could swim across the slough, walk over the peninsula and swim across the bay to the marina. He could then find someone to bring him back to the boat. We tossed a coin to determine who'd swim and who'd stay in the boat with Dorothy. I won the toss and chose to swim. My friend wasn't happy about staying with a woman about to have a baby. I was gone a little over an hour. Dorothy said our friend kept asking her how she felt about every ten minutes. He sure was happy to see me returning with the gas.

With the larger motor we could discard the surfboard and start water-skiing. There was just one problem. The new motor didn't have an electric starter. The only way to start it was with the pull rope. When you came from full throttle to idle, you had to do so slowly or the motor would stall. If I fell when Dorothy was pulling me on the skis, she'd often stall the motor. She didn't have enough strength to get it restarted. I had to swim back to the boat, start the motor and then jump back into the water to continue skiing.

Dorothy decided our problems were caused by the fact that we hadn't named the boat. I told her I'd agree with whatever name she decided on and put it on the side of the boat. A few days later she came to me and said we'd call the boat *Lil'Headache.* She felt this was an appropriate name because of all the troubles we'd had with the boat. After I put the name on the vessel, whenever we were on the water, people would comment on it. They'd say it was a very appropriate name.

One of our favorite places to go water-skiing was on the Columbia River near the Portland airport. There was a long sandy beach where the boats could be pulled on shore. We'd build a fire on the beach from driftwood and stay on into the evening. Just downstream there was a popular fishing hole where fishermen anchored off shore, hoping to catch a salmon.

One afternoon we were water-skiing with another couple. We'd finished skiing for the day and were relaxing around the fire. We watched a beautiful wooden cabin cruiser go by and head for the fishing hole and set anchor. A little later we looked downstream and saw smoke coming from the wooden cruiser. Then we saw a man standing on the bow as flames came from the back of the boat. The man jumped overboard. We took one of our boats and headed downstream to rescue him. By the time we arrived he was exhausted and incoherent. Luckily he was wearing a life jacket! We tried to pull him into the boat but he was a big man and too heavy to lift. The only thing we could do was drag him to shore and pull him onto the beach. While the man regained his strength, we watched that beautiful wooden boat burn to the waterline. Someone else came to shore in his dinghy to inform us he'd radioed the Coast Guard and they were on their way.

The owner of the burning boat told us he didn't have insurance and that it was his fault it had caught fire. He said he'd set anchor and turned off the engine. He then discovered he'd drifted past the hole. He knew that when he shut down the engine it was necessary to pull the throttle all the way back. If he didn't, the carburetor would drip gas into the bilge. He thought this was what happened. He was going to reset the anchor and started the engine without turning on the bilge blower to exhaust the fumes. A spark from starting the engine ignited the fumes.

In the late fifties my parents sold the Chris-Craft and bought a smaller 22 foot outboard cabin cruiser. It was powered with twin 40 horsepower outboard motors and had a top speed of twenty knots. In those days that made it a very fast boat.

This boat was named the *Lilly B.* It came complete with a trailer which meant that it could be towed to Ilwaco for the fall fishing season and to other places further away. This was not only quicker but less expensive.

One summer Dorothy and I thought it would be nice to take the *Lilly B* on a trip north of Seattle and explore the waters around Whidbey Island. At that time we were living in St. Helens, Oregon. We invited friends, Don and Lavenia Wilson, to make the trip with us. After a few weeks of planning and preparation, we were ready to go. We loaded the boat onto the trailer, and using the Wilson's 1955 Ford, we headed for the town of Mukilteo, Washington. The plan was to launch at the public launching ramp in Mukilteo and start our exploration from there.

We left St Helens a little later in the day than we'd originally planned. This was before the I-5 freeway so the main route to Seattle was highway 99. Because of our late start, we arrived in Seattle during the Boeing aircraft plant night shift change. Don was driving and there were cars and pedestrians coming at us from all directions. I was in the front seat reading the map and trying to determine which way to go and what lane we needed. With that big boat behind us, it was very hard for Don to see when he needed to make a lane change. We had people yelling at us and cars honking their horns for us to get out of their way. Somehow we made it through that mess and finally arrived at the launching ramp in Mukilteo around one o'clock in the morning.

The four of us were dead tired from the long and tiring drive, so we just parked the rig in the parking lot and crawled up into the boat and went to bed. It was just becoming daylight when I was awakened by a lot of noise outside. I sat up in bed and looked out the cabin window. I couldn't believe what I saw. There were cars and trucks with boat trailers parked all around us. The area was alive with people launching boats because, as we found later, it was the peak of the salmon season. I jumped out of bed and immediately started getting everyone up. We had to move soon or we would be blocked in by parked cars and trailers. We all got up and put the car in line to the launching ramp. We finally managed to launch the boat and then made arrangements to park the car and trailer while we were gone. After a quick breakfast aboard the boat, we headed up Possession Sound towards Whidbey Island.

We had a great time exploring the waters around Whidbey Island, including Holms Harbor and Penn Cove. While in Penn Cove, we toured the little town of Coupeville and all the heritage buildings.

One day we anchored off a beach in Saratoga Passage and took the dinghy ashore to dig clams. While there, we noticed people in their dinghies, drifting along in shallow water, catching something with salmon dip nets. Upon further inspection, we found they were catching crab: As the shadow from the dinghy drifted over the seaweed hiding the crab, they would come out and run along the bottom. As they scooted along, if you were quick enough, you could catch them with the net. The trick was being quick enough. Don and I tried for almost an hour and didn't catch a single crab.

Our vacation time was almost up so we decided to head back toward Mukilteo and the launching ramp. We thought we would make one more stop on the way back so we went into the public dock in Everett, Washington and took moorage for one night.

That was when we were visited by the little black cloud. We had decided that for something to do, we would go uptown to a movie. We were told it was several blocks away. Since it was raining at the time, we decided to call a taxi. We felt we couldn't afford a taxi both ways, but with the rain we would take the taxi there and hope that the rain would stop by the time the movie was over. When we came out of the theatre it was still raining as heavily as before.

As previously decided, we headed back to the boat on foot. I was wearing glasses and with the heavy rain, I couldn't see where I was going. I took them off and put them in my shirt pocket inside my jacket. When we arrived back at the boat, I bent over to unzip the back curtain. I heard something hit the deck and then splash into the water and I realized my glasses had fallen out of my pocket.

The next morning we found that it was a very low tide, so Don suggested we try to retrieve my glasses. I took one of the fishing rods and tied two large salmon lures to the line. These lures had two treble hooks each. I started walking up and down the dock alongside the boat dragging the lures in hopes of snagging my glasses. After several passes without success, I decided to give up. Don said that because of the way the tide was running last night, my glasses may have drifted further away than we thought. He took the rod and started dragging further down the dock. After the third try, he hooked my glasses.

Now that I could see again, we left Everett and headed for the launching ramp. Then the little black cloud came for another visit. We were going down Possession Sound heading for Mukilteo. The wind was blowing at about fifteen knots and we were heading directly into it. Our dinghy was an eight foot sabot type boat. We didn't have any place to carry it on board so we were towing it behind us. When we slowed down to come into the dock at Mukilteo I looked back and the dinghy was full of water and just barely afloat. We discovered the pounding it had taken traveling through the rough water, had worked the bottom loose from the keel. Fortunately, it was the end of our trip, so we could wait until we got home to do the needed repairs.

As with any boater we all get what we call "foot-ites". Not too long after Dorothy and I were married, I had a chance to buy a 23 foot cabin cruiser. This boat was an old double end life boat. It had a plywood hull and was powered by a Willys Jeep engine, the same as the one my parents had earlier. This boat didn't have a gear box so the drive shaft was attached directly to the engine. That meant you had to be pointed in the right direction before starting the engine, as well as turning the engine off at the right time when docking. It also had an ugly box for a cabin that was made of pressboard and was rapidly falling apart. The asking price was a hundred dollars.

I somehow talked Dorothy into letting me buy this boat with the idea that we could have it hauled out, put into her mother's barn where I could work on it under cover and as our money allowed. I drew up some plans for a new more attractive looking cabin with a nice interior lay out. I also picked up a marine gear that could be installed later. That would give the boat a forward, neutral, and reverse.

I had the new cabin almost finished and was getting ready to work on the interior when we lost everything. On October 12, 1962 there was a storm that blew through the Northwest with hurricane force winds. These winds were more that mom's old barn could stand and the whole barn came down on top of our unfinished cabin cruiser. It not only crushed the cabin but also knocked the boat off the blocks and one of the upright support poles went through the hull and broke one of the engine stringers.

I managed to get some of my money back by selling the engine and gear box. The hull was donated to a local church that used it as a display depicting Noah's Ark promoting their Sunday school.

In 1964, after losing the boat in the wind storm, I decided to build a new boat. There was a boat builder in North Portland called Clippercraft Boat Builders. They produced a line of plywood boats ranging in size from sixteen to twenty-two feet. These boats were sold either complete or at any stage of construction. They also supplied some models in a pre-cut kit form.

I decided to build the eighteen-foot open runabout model from the kit. I cleared out our garage and spent most of the next year building our new boat. One thing needed to build a boat is a type of cradle called a jig. As the frames are assembled they are placed at a designated position on the jig. One evening, as I was working on assembling the jig, I was using two pieces of two-by-six for longitudinal stringers and tried to get them level on the uneven garage floor. Instead of taking the time to get my hand plane, I pulled out my pocket knife and was shaving some of the wood from the corner of the jig. I was pulling with the knife blade when it suddenly slipped and the tip of the blade drove into the palm of my hand. I ran into the house, grabbed a towel and wrapped it around my hand. Dorothy decided we should head to the emergency at the nearest hospital.

When we arrived the doctor's at first thought I'd tried to commit suicide by cutting my wrist, but then they found the cut was in my hand and not my wrist. Finally, after two hours in emergency, I was sent home with five stitches in my hand. I went to bed but couldn't sleep because of the pain: the hospital had neglected to give me some pain killers.

By seven o clock in the morning my hand was so

swollen, it had almost doubled in size. The pain was horrible. Dorothy called our family doctor at his home and explained the situation. He said to meet him at his office in a half hour. When we arrived, he took a scalpel and cut two of the stitches to open the wound. There was a big rush of blood and a great relief from the pain. The doctor discovered that I had cut a blood vessel and the hospital hadn't tied it off before stitching up the wound!

While building the new boat, I started looking for a motor. I wanted something that would be suitable for the size of boat I was building. I found a V-four, 75 horsepower Evinrude that had a damaged power head. I hoped that I could find another motor of the same model that had a damaged lower unit. A friend of mine was an outboard motor mechanic at the local marina. One day he told me his shop had ordered in a new V-four power head for a customer. They then discovered the customer's old power head could be repaired. Rather than pay the shipping charges to return the new power head, they would sell it to me at dealer cost. I bought the power head and installed it on my motor and got a new outboard motor for less than half price.

The new boat was launched in the summer of 1965. We named her the *Da-Na-Do-Les*, a name derived from our first names, David, Nancy, Dorothy and Les. Behind the helm seat, I had built a small galley consisting of a sink, a two burner stove and a built-in ice box under the counter.

Da Nan Do Les

One Saturday afternoon we decided to go for a boat ride and have dinner aboard. Dorothy made some potato salad and prepared some hamburger patties to cook on the stove. We left the marina and headed down river for a few miles. We found a sandy beach where we pulled the boat onto shore. Dorothy was getting ready to start cooking hamburgers when she discovered we had forgotten to bring a frying pan. At first we tried using a flattened bean can but it wouldn't get hot enough because of the air space between the two sides of the can. Then I got an idea. We had a one gallon metal bucket aboard. Why couldn't we fry the meat in the bottom of the bucket.

Dorothy said, "We can't use that. It's our pee bucket."

"I'm hungry and so are the kids and we're two hours from home," I replied.

I took the bucket ashore and gave it a good scrubbing with some clean sand. I then brought it back aboard and sterilized it with boiling water. Dorothy fried the hamburgers using the bucket as a frying pan. From then on whenever someone had the urge, they'd say "pass me the frying pan".

Chapter Two:

The Learning Experience

When Dorothy and I moved to the lower mainland of Vancouver in 1969, we brought the *Da-Na-Do-Les* with us. It was primarily built for use on the Columbia River and not really suited for the open, rough waters around Vancouver.

One sunny summer weekend we thought it would be nice to go salmon fishing. I had talked to some of the locals and learned about a style of fishing called mooching. We were told that a good place to mooch would be an area called The Gap near Gibsons on the Sunshine Coast. I took the whole family and we pulled the boat to the launching ramp in False Creek. We launched and headed for Gibsons to find the gap. We were told to go to a place called Smitty's Marina to pick up some herring for bait and then anchor in the gap. We found Smitty's Marina and asked the attendant for a dozen herring. We were surprised when he came back to the boat with a net filled with a dozen wiggly live herring and asked, "Where are you going to keep them"? We didn't realize that we were to fish with live herring and keep the bait alive for it to be effective. We had a small sink and counter built in behind the helm seat, so we decided to fill the sink with salt water and put the herring in the sink. Then the attendant took me into the store and spent some time showing me what I needed for hooks and sinkers. He also explained how to attach the bait to the hooks. We bought the proper gear and headed out to anchor in The Gap with hopes of catching a salmon or two.

That's when we experienced surprise number two. We had no idea that the depth would be 100 feet or more. When we boated on the Columbia River, the water depth was always around 25 to 30 feet deep unless you were out in the ship channel and nobody ever anchored out there. We were not equipped with a depth sounder because when boating on the Columbia River there was little need for one. We found what looked to be a good place to try fishing and started to drop the anchor. We were surprised to find that 50 feet of anchor rope was not nearly enough to reach bottom. With all of our anchor line out we were still drifting toward the Strait of Georgia. Our only alternative was to try mooching while drifting.

After drifting out of The Gap and running back in several times we were running low on fuel. We also discovered our live bait was no longer live because we had forgotten to keep the water in the sink fresh! By this time it was getting late in the day and we had to get back to False Creek before dark. We went back to Smitty's to top up the fuel tank and headed for home empty handed but with a lot more knowledge than we had started with. In the future, after buying 200 feet of anchor line, we had many more fishing trips with much better success.

We were then paid another visit from the little black cloud when we took the Da-Nan-Do-Les over to Plumper Cove Marine Park. We were told about this nice Marine Park on Keats Island so we decided to go check it out and spend a weekend camping. I had bought a chart of Howe Sound earlier and studied it before we left. I found that in a seventeen foot boat it is rather difficult to keep the chart open in front of you while under way.

I thought it would be shorter if we went on the east side of Pasley Island, out into Barfleur Passage, over to the gap and into Plumper Cove on Keats Island. We were scooting along at a pretty good clip and just going around the top end of Pasley Island when suddenly BANG! The outboard motor kicked up and the revs went wild. After shutting down the engine, I looked over the back and discovered we had broken a sizeable piece off one blade of the propeller.

I then got out the chart and found that there was a submerged rock just off the top end of Pasely Island and we had found it the hard way. I thought that the propeller was still useable if we took it slow and easy, so we headed on towards Plumper Cove. I put the motor into gear but as soon as I tried to apply any throttle, it would just rev up and act as if it was in neutral. That was when I discovered that I had torn the center rubber hub loose in the propeller and the best I could go was about 1500 RPM. In those days I did not carry an extra propeller with me, so the rest of the weekend we traveled along at a grueling five knots.

On another occasion, around the end of June, David and I launched at False Creek and took the boat to the Gibsons area to do some salmon fishing. We found that other boaters receive visits from the little black cloud also. We stayed out a little later than we should have. By the time we headed back to False Creek it was starting to get dark. On our way across the south end of Bowen Island we saw a good sized power boat with a man standing on the bow waving a red life jacket. We pulled along side to see what the trouble was. He told us that he had engine trouble and had run his battery down trying to get it started. We didn't have a radio on our boat and his radio wasn't working. This was before the time of cell phones, so we had no way of contacting the Coast Guard. The man and his wife were the only two aboard and their boat was drifting towards the rocks on Bowen Island. We had no choice but to take them in tow.

This boat was in the 30 foot range and we were in a small eighteen foot outboard. They wanted us to tow them to Thunderbird Marina in West Vancouver. By the time we finally got their boat hooked up and in tow it was around 7:30 in the evening. With our small outboard boat pulling that large cabin cruiser we were only making about four or five knots and it was getting progressively darker.

When David and I hadn't arrived home on time and Dorothy hadn't heard from us, she started to get worried. She called the Coast Guard but they informed her that they wouldn't send out a search party until she drove down to the launching ramp to make sure the truck and trailer were still there. They reasoned that too many people would come in from a fishing trip, stop at the local pub and neglect to call home. As soon as David and I got the boat secured at Thunderbird Marina the first thing we did was find the nearest phone and call home. We managed to catch Dorothy just as she was getting ready to leave the house. She then called the Coast Guard back to inform them what had happened.

By this time it was around ten o'clock on a Sunday night and the next day was a school day. Our boat was in West Vancouver and our trailer at the False Creek launching ramp in Vancouver. The people we rescued said they would drive us to our car. We made arrangements with Fisherman's Cove to leave the boat for the night, agreeing to come back the next day to pick it up.

All the way to the launching ramp, this couple kept insisting on stopping someplace to buy us dinner. I insisted that we had to get home so David could get some sleep before school the next day. Finally, we were dropped off at the truck and trailer and made it home sometime after midnight.

The next day, a friend and I went back to Thunderbird

Marina to get the boat. There is no launch ramp at Thunderbird Marina, hence I had to run the boat around to Sewell's launch ramp at Horseshoe Bay, while my friend drove the truck and trailer around. After that trip Dorothy and I agreed that we had a little black cloud following me around when I'm out on the water.

Another visit from the little black cloud occurred when our son David and I launched the boat at Sunset Marina and headed towards Gibsons for a day of salmon fishing. Rounding the north end of Bowen Island the water started to get a little rough. By the time we crossed the top of Collingwood Channel and rounded the north end of Keats Island, the wind was blowing at about fifteen knots. This made it too rough to fish in The Gap, so we went back and trolled along the north end of Keats Island.

Suddenly, David hooked a fish but he didn't think it was a salmon. He said he could feel something on the line but it was like pulling a heavy boot off the bottom. After working at it for almost a half an hour, we both looked over the side of the boat and saw the ugliest fish head we had ever seen. It had a mouth that looked like it could swallow the whole boat. We managed to get the fish into the boat and, upon checking the fishing regulations, found that we had caught a ling cod. That fish weighed in at a little less than 20 pounds.

We fished for another hour or so as the wind kept getting stronger and the seas grew rougher so we decided to head for home. We were about half way to the marina and our poor little boat was really taking a beating. I then heard David yell that we were taking on a lot of water. I went back and pulled the drain plug and put David to work bailing. Bailing as fast as he could, he was having a hard time keeping up with the incoming water. We made it to the launching ramp and I ran to get the car and trailer. By the time I got the trailer backed into the water, the boat was almost half sunk! We finally got the boat onto the trailer and discovered the boat had been pounding so hard that the plywood came loose from the keel. The water was pouring out from the bottom of the boat like a waterfall. At that time we decided that if we were going to continue to boat around the area, we needed a bigger, more suitable boat.

Chapter Three:

The New Boat

In the summer of 1972, we bought a 23 foot 1969 Reinell hardtop express cruiser.

Coming from the little eighteen foot open runabout to the Reinell felt like we were running the Queen Mary. The new boat had a big V-berth up forward, a galley with a two burner alcohol stove, a sink with a fresh water pump and an ice box for a refrigerator. It also had a head up under the V- berth. All four of us could sleep comfortably in it by folding down the dinette table and converting the motor box into a bunk. We named this boat *Time Out*. We procured in-the-water moorage at a seaplane dock in coal harbor, near where Canada Place now sits.

With the bigger boat we felt better about going farther afield. However, the little black cloud decided that it would follow us in the new boat as well. We bought the necessary charts and decided to spend a weekend in the Gulf Islands.

Dorothy and I had both taken the power squadron course while living in Oregon but that course was based on the Columbia River. They have a small tide change on the Columbia but nothing close to the amount of change in British Columbia waters. Our first experience with B.C. tides was when we were in Genoa Bay across from Cowichan Bay. We headed out from our moorage in Coal Harbor and navigated through the First Narrows. Our plan was to head for the Gulf Islands via Active Pass. As we started across the Strait of Georgia it was a bit hazy and we were unable to see all the way across to the Gulf Islands. I had installed and calibrated a new compass in the boat. Calling upon my Power Squadron experience and using the new compass I set a course for Active Pass.

We were told that in most of the Gulf Island anchorages, we'd require a dinghy to get onto shore. Therefore, we borrowed a seven foot Sport Yak dinghy from a fellow boater and tied it to the hard top. As we traveled out into the Strait, the wind became stronger and the seas grew rougher.

As this was our first time across we thought this was normal, so we slowed down but kept going. We then discovered that the ropes securing the dinghy were coming loose. I stopped, put the engine in neutral and, with the boat rocking from side to side in the waves, I went up on top and managed to secure the dinghy.

As we made progress across the Strait, we could see the Gulf Islands ahead of us, but it was hard to determine the entrance to Active Pass. As any boater can tell you when you are in poor weather conditions, it is hard to trust your compass and stay on course.

However, I did trust my compass and followed the course originally laid out. It was not long before we could see that we were right on target and headed into the entrance to Active Pass.

We navigated our way through Active Pass, across Trincomali Channel and made our way into Ganges Harbor. With great relief, we took moorage at the Ganges Government Dock and spent the rest of the afternoon relaxing.

The next day we came out of Ganges Harbor, down Swanson Channel and around into Satellite Channel. We headed up Satellite Channel and into Genoa Bay. After surveying the situation, we decided to take anchorage in the head of the bay for the night. I checked the tide book to make sure we had enough water under us to allow for the tide drop.

After dinner, our son David put out the crab trap and we all went to bed. When I got up the next morning, I went out back to check things. Looking over the side, I found that we were within about six inches of sitting on top of our crab trap! Luckily I had lifted the outdrive the night before because we had less than a foot of water under us.

Time Out

Our first year with the Reinell, we gained a lot of experience. Even with all the bad experiences and a few mechanical breakdowns, I was able to repair the damage myself and we always managed to make it back home. Dorothy said she still thought that we had a little black cloud following us around and every once in a while he dumped on us.

We made some new friends through my place of employment. This couple owned a summer cabin in Halfmoon Bay on the Sunshine Coast. They said we should get together sometime and spend a weekend at their cabin. Later we decided to do so. The plan was for this couple, their daughter and our family to take our boat and meet some other people from work at the cabin in Halfmoon Bay.

With the boat fully loaded and the fuel tanks full we headed out of Cole Harbor. After we came through First Narrows, I gave the boat full throttle to get up to cruising speed. No matter how hard I tried, the boat wouldn't get up on a plane. Before, when we gave the engine full throttle, we were up on a plane quite fast. We would cruise along at about 18 to 20 knots. I tried moving people forward but it still didn't help. I concluded that we had too much weight in the boat so we ran along at about 8 knots all the way to Halfmoon Bay. Because of our slow speed, we were about three hours late getting to our destination. When we did arrive, the other people were no-where to be found. We waited for them at the cabin for a little over an hour, but they still didn't arrive. Because they were coming by car and had more room, we had previously decided to have them bring all the food for the weekend. The nearest place to buy groceries was at Madeira Park in Pender Harbor, several miles away. Without land transportation the only thing we could do was take the boat all the way to Pender Harbor and back to buy food for the weekend.

We still had an enjoyable weekend at the cabin. We did some fishing and even ate some fresh oysters picked off the beach. After arriving back home, we contacted the others. They said they had arrived in Halfmoon Bay several hours ahead of us but didn't know which cabin we were staying in. After waiting in the car for a couple hours, they had decided that we were not coming and went back home.

The next weekend, I was at the boat talking to some people on the dock. I said something about not getting the speed out of the boat like I used to and was thinking about getting a different propeller. These people said maybe I should take a look at the growth on the bottom.

They asked, "When was the last time you painted the bottom with antifouling paint?"

Coming from the Columbia River with its fresh water I asked, "What do you mean antifouling paint?"

That was another lesson learned the hard way. The following weekend we put the boat on the trailer and brought it home. The bottom of that boat was almost solid barnacles and mussels. I then made the mistake of crawling under the boat and scraping off all the growth and letting it fall on the ground in the driveway. The stink from all that mess almost got us kicked out of the neighborhood!

With the bottom cleaned and a fresh coat of antifouling paint, the boat was back up to speed without installing a new propeller.

After a few trips on our own and some lessons learned, we saw an ad in the local boating magazine for membership to a local boating club. The ad was for the Vancouver Cruising Club stating that they were a boating club dedicated to family cruising with other boaters. This sounded good to us so we called and were told that they were having a cruise to Center Bay on Gambier Island in a couple of weeks. It was suggested that we join them and meet some of the members. When the weekend came, we loaded the boat and headed out to find Center Bay on Gambier Island. We were told to look for a 22 foot cabin cruiser called the *Miako*.

On the day we left Coal Harbor, it was raining so hard the visibility was down to less than a mile. We cruised out under the First Narrows Bridge and made our way around Point Atkinson. We went up Queen Charlotte Channel, around Hood Point and finally found our way into Center Bay but we couldn't find a boat called "Miako". After cruising around in the bay for some time, we finally saw three boats tied alongside a log boom. We motored over to see if these were the people we were looking for. Indeed, they were from the Vancouver Cruising Club, but because of the bad weather the *Miako* didn't come out that weekend. We stayed for the rest of the day, but with the heavy rain everyone was confined to their boats. The weekend was a total washout and everyone left to go home early so, we didn't get to meet many people on that cruise.

We were told that the next cruise would be to Secret Cove on the Sunshine Coast for the Labor Day long weekend, and we should join the annual club fishing derby.

We had been to Halfmoon Bay so we felt sure that we could find Secret Cove. With our family of four and all the gear needed for the long weekend, we headed up the Sunshine Coast to find Secret Cove. We found out why they call it "Secret" Cove. We came out of Welcome Pass and went sailing right by the entrance to Secret Cove and soon found ourselves in Pender Harbor. After inquiring at Irving's Landing we were given directions on how to find Secret Cove.

That weekend we did get to meet a few of the members of the boating club and found them to be a great bunch of people, some of whom we still associate with today. We met one couple, and upon getting to know them a little better, we found that their boating experiences were very similar to ours.

Their names were Darrel and Wendy and they owned a 20 foot Glasstron cabin cruiser. They had also experienced breakdowns and a few misjudgments. Darrel said that he thought the same little black cloud had been following them around as well. We got together and decided to name the little black cloud Harold. After that, when we said that we had a visit from Harold, we all knew what was meant.

Darrel and Wendy related to us the story about when Harold had paid them a visit on an overnight trip with the family. They had two small children, a boy and a girl. The younger was the girl whose name was Lisa. Their little boat only had the one bunk up forward under the bow. The sleeping arrangement were: the two adults and the boy would sleep on the v-birth and Lisa, who was about two years old at the time, would sleep on the floor below them.

One night, all four of them had been out on an overnight stay. They were all in bed and enjoying a good night's sleep when Lisa woke them up crying. Darrel kept telling her to be quiet and go back to sleep. The next thing he knew, Lisa was trying to get up and crawl into their bunk. Not having enough room in the v-birth for both children, Darrel reached over and pushed Lisa back down into her bed. He then discovered that he was pushing her down into a pool of water. He immediately jumped out of bed and put his feet into about six inches of water. They later discovered that the weight of all four of them in the forward part of the boat had allowed the discharge of the toilet to go below the water line and they had not closed off the outlet valve. The water was feeding back through the toilet and into the boat.

Another time, we had just come back from a weekend outing and were sitting at our moorage in Coal Harbor busy putting things away. I looked up and saw a small boat about 22 feet long, with Oregon license numbers on the bow, pulling into the dock. The skipper asked us how to get to Pender Harbor on the Sunshine Coast from there. We looked at this boat and couldn't believe what we saw. Aboard was a mother, a father, two children and a grandmother. They had luggage and crab traps tied down on the top of the cabin and so many items inside the little cabin that they could hardly move around. I asked the skipper to get his charts and I would show him how to find Pender Harbor. He went to his boat and came back with a Shell Oil road map. They had launched their boat in Anacortes, Washington and traveled all the way through the San Juan Islands, the Gulf Islands and across the strait to Vancouver Harbor following a road map! I took him up to the local marine store and showed him the charts he needed to buy to get to where they wanted to go, as well as the charts needed to get back to Anacortes. We stood on the dock waving goodbye and shaking our heads as they headed out of Vancouver Harbor, hoping they would have a safe trip.

In the 1960's and early 1970's *The Vancouver Sun* newspaper sponsored a salmon derby each summer. There was a program where you could offer your boat and get paid to take people out for the day to fish in the derby. Now that I'd had some success with my salmon fishing, I thought I would make a few bucks and try my hand at being a fishing guide.

Harold hit at the most inopportune time. I put my name in for the program and was given two guys from the U.S. I picked them up at the Bay Shore Inn early on the morning of the derby. I put some coffee on the stove and after we all had a cup, we headed out for a day of salmon fishing.

My plan was to run out and troll along the bottom of Bowen Island and work my way towards Gibsons. As we were coming around Point Atkinson the engine started to overheat. Later, I found that I had run over a plastic bag and it was blocking the cooling water intake. I managed to limp into Thunderbird Marina where I went on land, phoned the Sun Derby people, and told them about my problem. I informed them that I could repair the problem but it could take up to three hours to put a new impeller in the water pump. They decided it would be best if they sent out another boat to take on my passengers.

When I came back from making the phone call to inform the guys what was happening, I found the galley in a big mess. They had decided that, while I was gone, they would heat up the coffee. Not knowing how to light an alcohol stove they had just pumped it up, turned it on and lit it. If you have ever used an alcohol stove you know it has to be primed before lighting. If not primed it will flare up with a very high flame and keep getting higher if not turned off right away. That is exactly what happened, so they panicked, grabbed the fire extinguisher and cut loose. They emptied the extinguisher all over the stove and the whole galley including the windows, walls, as well as the ceiling!

After the other boat came and took these guys off fishing, I repaired the water pump and headed for home. It took me the rest of the day to clean up the mess in the galley and I never did get the fluid cleaned out of the stove burners. I finally had to replace both burners in the stove.

This was only the beginning of my problems. In the next few months we had to be towed in two different times because of engine overheating. The impeller shaft in the sea water pump kept breaking. After replacing the shaft two times, I discovered the brass housing of the pump had gotten so hot from the first time it overheated, that it had warped out of shape and the shaft could not run true. This caused it to keep breaking.

After replacing the complete water pump, I had no more overheating problems.

This was the first and last time I did fishing charters!

Chapter Four:

Going the Distance

In the summer of '74 we really had a problem with "Harold" following us around. It was our first trip north.

We started the trip by joining a club cruise to Plumper Cove on Keats Island for the weekend. Prior to that, I had been having trouble with my engine developing a slight miss at higher speeds. I had gone through the carburetor and fuel system as well as checking the electrical and couldn't find the problem. It was difficult to find because it wasn't consistent enough to pin down. While we were at Plumper Cove, someone suggested that maybe I had a bad hydraulic valve lifter causing the problem. My friend Darrel said he had an extra set of valve lifters in his garage at home. He could call his neighbor and have him bring them, along with any other parts needed, out to Horseshoe Bay.

It was decided that Darrel and I would start dismantling the engine to get to the lifters and my son, David, would go to Horseshoe Bay in his seven foot dinghy that had a six horsepower outboard, to pick up the parts. When David came back with the parts, his boat had a lot of water in it. He had run into some pretty rough water and took quite a bit over the bow. He was proud that he had made it back safely!

Darrel and Wendy had sold the little 20 Foot Glasstron and purchased a 24 foot Fiberform hardtop express cruiser. This boat was about the same size as the *Time Out* with almost the same interior lay-out. It was powered with a Chrysler V-8 engine on a Volvo outdrive. They named this boat the *Li-Bri II.* Darrel was also having troubles of his own. The pulley on the alternator kept coming loose. Along with working on my engine we were also trying to get his alternator pulley fixed. We finally got my engine back together that evening only to discover that the new valve lifters did not help at all. We then decided that we would go north anyway and try to live with the problem.

All of our fellow club members thought we were crazy for doing major engine work like that out in the field but we wanted to get started on our trip north. They also thought we were really out of our minds to take a trip that long without properly running engines.

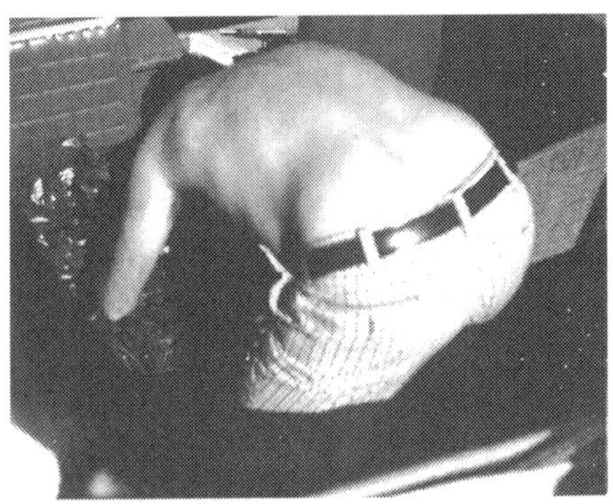

Engine Repair

One thing we wanted to do on that trip was go to Princess Louisa Inlet. Darrel was still having trouble with his alternator pulley, so we decided to make the run up to Princes Louisa on our own. The plan was that we would meet up with the *Li-Bre II* somewhere around Nelson Island on our way back down.

This was the first of two trips we took in the *Time Out* to Princes Louisa Inlet and Harold followed us there on both occasions. Going up Jervis Inlet has some of the most beautiful scenery we ever saw in all our boating experiences. Once you pass Egmont and head up Prince of Wales Reach, the channel starts to narrow and you're traveling between high mountains on both sides. As you round the corner and start up Princess Royal Reach, the channel becomes even more narrow and the scenery more spectacular. Around the next bend is Queen's Reach and the mountains are higher and the water is unbelievably clear and blue. Then suddenly on your Starboard side is the narrow opening of Malibu Rapids, which is the entrance taking you into Princess Louisa Inlet.

That's where we met Harold again. Just as we were going through Malibu Rapids, I happened to look down at the instruments and noticed the alternator was not showing a charge. We continued to the end of the inlet and anchored to the left of the dock where the waterfall empties into the inlet. Upon inspection, I discovered a broken belt on the alternator. I always carry spare belts with me, so after replacing the belt, we were good to go.

We stayed the night at our anchorage and the next day took the dinghy over to the dock. As you near the head of Princess Louisa Inlet, you can see the falls where they come out of the forest and cascade down the mountainside. Standing at the base of the falls and watching the water drop over 100 feet off the cliff with the spray coming off the falls on you, that's when you realize how magnificent the falls are.

Li-Bri II and Time Out

We discovered that Harold visits other boats besides ours. We returned down Jervis inlet to meet with the *Li-Bre II* at Nelson Island. We found them anchored in Blind Bay so we came alongside and rafted for the evening. After dinner the children asked if they could take the dinghy and go exploring. We said "yes", but be back before dark. They were only gone a short time when they came rushing back to tell us about this big boat they had seen sitting on a rock. We had to go and see what they were talking about. Upon arriving at the entrance to Blind Bay between Hardy and Nelson Islands, there was a boat close to 50 feet long sitting half submerged on a rock. Someone had done a poor job of navigation and run onto one of the rocks guarding the entrance. It was a shame to see such a beautiful boat sitting under water.

The following day we left Blind Bay and continued our trip north. We ventured out into Malaspina Strait heading toward Powell River. Traveling on the inside of Texada Island, we went past Grief Point and into Westview Harbor for a fuel stop. After topping up the fuel and water tanks we continued past Savary Island and Lund, inside the Copeland Islands, around Sarah Point and finally into Desolation Sound.

We had all read the book *"The Curve of Time"* by Wylie Blanchet about her adventures in her little boat called "Caprice". We were intrigued by the tale of her going into Melanie Cove in Prideaux Haven and meeting the old hand logger called Mike. She talked about the little cabin Mike had built at the end of the cove and how he had planted all the fruit trees around the cabin. We anchored in the end of Melanie Cove and put the dinghies down. Rowing ashore, we went to see if we could find the old cabin. We were disappointed by the fact that the cabin was gone. However, we were pleased to find a lot of the apple trees Mike had planted. You could also see where he had built the terraces around the cabin and we found the foundation where the cabin once stood.

That evening it was clear and warm, so we were all sitting in the back of the boats enjoying the stars and watching the odd satellite blink its way across the sky. Suddenly something unexpected happened. The Northern Lights came on overhead and put on a spectacular display for us! We watched them for a good fifteen to twenty minutes before they disappeared into the night.

We then decided to go to Squirrel Cove on Cortes Island. Dorothy and I had to make a stop at Refuge Cove so the *Li-Bre II* went ahead to find us a place to anchor. When we came past the public dock at Squirrel Cove, we called the *LiBre II* on the radio to find out where they were. They replied “We are in row two space number six”. As we came through the gap going into the cove we could see what they were talking about. There were wall to wall boats, all with anchors set off the bow and stern tied to shore.

Squirrel Cove is a well-protected anchorage with lots of things to do. There is a small café on the west side of the bay that serves a great smoked salmon dinner. You can also take the path through the forest and walk over to Von Donop Inlet. There is a salt water lagoon south east of the cove which, when the tide is high, you can run up the tidal creek with your dinghy. That’s where Harold struck our son. He was having a great time with his dinghy and outboard motor running up and down the creek going in and out of the lagoon. Unfortunately, he lost track of time and was not watching the tide. He was coming down the creek as the water was getting very shallow from the outgoing tide. He hit bottom with the motor which broke half of one blade off the propeller. That totally ruined his week. A young man with a dinghy and no outboard motor to run around in was likely to be a disaster.

Our next stop was Grace Harbor in Malaspina Inlet. We anchored in the bay and went on shore where we had a great time exploring the area and checking out all the old abandoned logging equipment. That evening we built a bonfire on shore and had a wiener and marshmallow roast. Everyone was having a good time except David. He was feeling down because of his broken motor.

The next day, we were so tired of hearing David complain, we looked on the chart and saw that there was a road from the public dock in Okeover Inlet that went to Lund. We decided to go to the public dock and Dorothy and Wendy would walk to Lund with the children and see if they could buy a new propeller. David was so upset that he kicked the broken propeller all the way down the road to Lund.

Darrel and I stayed with the boats. After about four hours we were beginning to wonder where the women were. We then discovered that the distance from the dock to Lund was a lot farther than we had expected. Thankfully they were given a ride from a nice person on the way back, or they might not have made it back before dark. The whole thing was a waste anyway because there wasn't any place in Lund that had a propeller to fit David's motor. I don't think that was one of his best summer holidays.

During that whole trip north, the engine would run well most of the time, and then suddenly it would start running rough. It would drop off a couple of hundred RPM. After that trip, I took the boat into a marine repair shop, hoping that they could find the problem. One of the mechanics came aboard and we took the boat for a run. Luckily, the engine started running rough as soon as we left the dock. The mechanic was back in the engine compartment and I was at the helm. Then he did something and the engine smoothed out right away. Next, he did something again and the roughness came back. He discovered that an electrical part mounted on the back of the engine had corroded. Once in a while the corrosion would short out against the engine. When the corrosion was cleaned off, the motor ran as it should.

Chapter Five:

Harold Goes To the San Juan Islands

The summer of 1975 was also the time of our first trip to the San Juan Islands. Yes, Harold followed us there too. Again, this trip was taken with Darrel and Wendy in their boat the *Li-Bre II*. In fact, we spent almost all of our summer holidays with the *Li-Bre II*.

We worked our way down through the Gulf Islands and cleared customs at Bedwell Harbor. We jokingly kept telling each other that when we crossed the boundary between the US and Canada in the middle of Haro Strait, we had to slow down and lift the outdrives to avoid getting caught on the boundary line. Dorothy and I cleared customs ahead of the *Li-Bre II* and headed across Haro strait. We were just starting down Spieden Channel, running alongside Stuart Island, when the *Li-Bre II* called us on the radio and Darrel said there was something wrong with the outdrive.

He said "The outdrive is making a loud grinding noise and I had to shut down".

Thinking back on the joke we had made about crossing Haro Strait, I called back and said, "Very funny. Now quit joking and let's get going".

Darrel said, "No, I'm serious. We really are broken

down. Come back and help us".

We turned around and went back to help. We took them in tow and pulled them to Roche Harbor on San Juan Island, because it was the nearest place to go. Wendy and their kids got in our boat while Darrel stayed aboard the *Li-Bre II* and sulked all the way to Roche Harbor. Darrel said that when we arrived at the marina, he could probably run his outdrive enough to maneuver his boat into a mooring slip. When we got to Roche Harbor, I called ahead on the radio and we were assigned mooring spots clear around on the inside of the marina. I pulled the *Li-Bre II* around and down toward our assigned spots, then turned the boat loose to let him get into his spot. Darrel started his engine and put it into gear but nothing happened. The engine revved up but he didn't move. When he looked down at the outdrive, he discovered the propeller was missing. It was there when we had taken them in tow, but during the tow, the prop nut had backed off and he'd lost it.

Li-Bri ll in Tow

That was not the only problem. On the way through the Gulf Islands we spent a day in Telegraph Harbor on Thetis Island. While sitting at the dock, a fellow came walking along looking at all the boats trying to find someone with a Volvo outdrive. He had ruined his propeller and didn't have a spare. So Darrel, being a nice guy, let this fellow borrow his spare propeller. Now Darrel had a broken outdrive and no propeller. Upon going to the store at the head of the dock, we were informed that there was no repair shop in Roche Harbor. The nearest place for repairs was Friday Harbor on the other side of the island. I had already towed their boat over six nautical miles and now we had another nine and a half nautical miles to get to Friday Harbor.

So away we went out of Roche Harbor, around the north end of San Juan Island, down San Juan Channel and into Friday Harbor. After arriving in Friday Harbor we found a repair shop that was capable of doing the necessary repairs, but they were very busy and would not be able to look at it until the next day. Having no choice, Darrel decided to wait and have the repairs done as soon as the mechanics were able. The repairmen wanted to put the boat on a trailer so it would be out of the water and near the shop. That meant Darrel and his family had to live on the boat while it was on shore. The shop set up a ladder system so they could get in and out of the boat, gave them a key to the washrooms, and saying they would get to the repair as soon as possible.

By the middle of the next afternoon the outdrive was removed and it was determined that one gear and some bearings needed to be replaced, but they would have to order the parts in from Seattle. They would be on the ferry the next afternoon. The mechanics could get everything back together and have the "Le-Bre II" back in the water within the next couple of days.

We decided to take everyone in our boat and go to Jones Island for the day. Everything we'd heard about Jones Island was true! There is a public dock in a very well protected bay with nice walking paths on the island. As we walked around the island we saw many deer that didn't seem at all afraid of us. It was a nice warm day and we all had a very enjoyable time while trying to forget our troubles. Early in the afternoon we headed back to Friday Harbor to get the *Li-Bre II* and finish our holiday.

Then Harold came for another visit. When we arrived back at the repair shop, we saw that the boat was still sitting on the trailer. Darrel went to check it out and was informed that Seattle had sent the wrong parts so they needed to re-order. With the weekend arriving they didn't expect parts until next Monday afternoon.

We decided to leave Friday Harbor and go to Deer Harbor for the weekend. We took both families in our boat and when we arrived at Deer Harbor, Darrel and his family rented a cabin for the weekend. We used the *Time Out* to explore the nearby islands. Making our weekend a little more enjoyable was a small restaurant at the head of the dock that made the biggest and best hamburgers we'd ever eaten.

On Monday afternoon we went back to Friday Harbor. The boat was still sitting in the same place with no outdrive attached. We were told that because it was Canadian built, the parts were only available in Canada. Darrel agreed to call the supplier in Vancouver, order the parts needed and have them sent to Sidney, where he could take the ferry from Friday Harbor to get them. They promised to have the parts in Sidney the next day. Darrel was on the morning ferry and back that afternoon with the correct parts and the shop had everything back together the following day, After being laid up for almost a week, we were finally on our way but with our holidays almost over, it was time to head for home.

When Darrel got home he found his spare prop and a case of beer sitting on his back porch.

CHAPTER SIX:

The San Juan's Again

Harold visited us again on a later trip to the San Juan Islands. Again we were with the Haines family in the *Li-Bre II*. We left Telegraph Harbor and headed south down Stuart Channel, through Sansum Narrows. We were rounding the south end of Saltspring Island into Satellite Channel when my engine started to overheat. I could keep the temperature down as long as I kept the engine under 2000 RPM. We decided to stop at Tsehum Harbor on Vancouver Island and take moorage for the day to see if we could determine why the engine was overheating. It didn't take long to discover that the problem was the exhaust manifolds. The risers were plugged where the cooling water exited into the muffler and kept the water from exiting the engine. I removed both risers, and while sitting at the dock with a screwdriver and coat hanger along with a fresh water hose, Darrel and I cleaned out both risers. I re-installed the risers and we had no further problems with overheating. On this trip we managed to get across Haro Strait with no outdrive problems.

Our first stop in the San Juan Islands was Reid Harbor on Stuart Island. Stuart Island has some nice hiking trails and interesting places to visit. There are quite a few people living there full time and, because of that, it has a small school that services Stuart Island and some of the adjacent islands. It reminded us of the old schools used in small towns of by-gone days. Because it was summer, we were not able to go inside, but from the outside it looked like it had two or three rooms. Also on the grounds is the original one room school that has been preserved as a museum.

Just as you come onto the grounds, there was a treasure chest under a large tree. In the chest were some tee-shirts with different designs on them. There was a sign on the tree saying that the tee-shirts were for sale and the funds were to go to the students to support their field trips. The shirts were sold on the honor system: you picked the design and size you wanted and left the money in the box. We bought a couple of shirts but didn't have the proper change so we followed the instructions on the sign and mailed them a check upon returning home.

We left Reid Harbor and headed down San Juan Channel toward Friday Harbor. Because of the previous time in the San Juan's, Darrel didn't want to stop in Friday Harbor. However, we found it necessary to make a stop to pick up supplies and refuel the boats. After arriving and being in a more relaxed mood, we enjoyed spending time looking around and doing some shopping.

From Friday Harbor we headed back up San Juan Channel, through Wasp Passage between Wasp Islands and Shaw Island, and went into Deer Harbor. Of course we had no trouble talking Darrel in going to Deer Harbor again for some of those big, delicious hamburgers.

We'd made arrangements earlier to meet another one of our boating friends in Garrison Bay on the west side of San Juan Island. We came out of Deer Harbor, navigated through North Pass, came across San Juan Channel and went around past Davison Head on the north end of San Juan Island, then headed into Roche Harbor. From Roche Harbor we went through Mosquito Pass and into Garrison Bay.

Garrison Bay is the site of English Camp where the British troops were garrisoned during the dispute over the boundary between Canada and the U.S. It is now a historical site operated by the U.S. Park Service. Several of the buildings and the grounds have been restored and you can tour the area including the cemetery where several people of that era are buried. There are also rangers on hand to explain about the history and show interpretive videos. We thoroughly enjoyed our stay there.

We found our friends waiting for us in Garrison Bay, so we came alongside and rafted to them. Their boat was a 22 foot carvel planked wooden boat built by Artcraft. They kept this boat on a trailer when not in use. Keeping a plank hull wooden boat out of the water is unwise because the planks will shrink when not submerged in water, then leak until the wood swells up again. That evening while rafted alongside we found we had chosen the wrong side. We were rafted on the port side which is the side of the bilge pump outlet. We didn't get much sleep that night because every five minutes or so our boat was being sprayed on the side by a stream of water coming from their bilge pump. From then on, we made sure that if rafted next to these friends we were always on the starboard side.

Our summer holiday time was coming to an end so it was time to head back home. Our friends in the Artcraft left and headed for Sidney to clear customs and head home. The Haines' and ourselves decided on the way home that we would spend a couple of nights in Fossil Bay on Sucia Island.

Before leaving San Juan Island, we wanted to visit some people we knew who lived in Mitchell Bay just around the corner from Garrison Bay. So the *Li-Bre II* headed off ahead while we stopped for a few hours to visit our friends. By the time we got under way, it was getting late in the afternoon.

We made our way back through Mosquito Pass, around the top of San Juan Island, and headed up President Channel. The wind had come up, so the seas were getting rough. As we came out of President Channel across the top of Orcas Island we were in the Strait of Georgia. The farther out in the Strait we got the rougher it became but we decided to tough it out and keep going. When we finally arrived in Fossil Bay where the *Li-Bre II* was waiting for us, the Haines' said they had given up on us because of the weather. They then looked and saw this little white spot with a lot of white water around it coming across the Strait. They decided it must be the *Time Out*. They couldn't believe we'd try to come across in such bad weather. We said "Why not? We've been in a lot worse seas than this".

Chapter Seven:

Harold Goes North Again

Harold also followed us on our second trip to Princess Louisa Inlet. In the summer of 1976 my mother and stepfather wanted to do some cruising with us. They owned a 24 -foot Reinell Command Bridge called *Mi-Lil 1* which they kept on a trailer. My mother had been to Princess Louisa Inlet some time back and wanted to go up there again.

It was decided that Mom and Milo would trailer their boat from Oregon and launch in Port Moody. We would then take the *Time Out* and along with the *Li-Bre II,* the three boats would run up the sunshine coast to Pender Harbor, then on up Jervis Inlet to Princess Louisa Inlet.

All was going fine until we came to Malibu rapids. The other two boats were ahead of us. We were on the end of the flood tide so we all headed through the rapids at the same time.

We were about half way through when suddenly my engine made a slight noise and dropped about 400 rpm. We made our way up to the head of the inlet and found moorage at the public floats below Chatterbox Falls. As I pulled the throttle back to an idle, the engine died. It would start but not idle. This led me to believe I had a fuel problem. I removed the carburetor, thinking it had dirt in it. Finding nothing wrong, I began replacing the carburetor. In the process, I stripped the threads where the fuel line connects to the carburetor. We were then almost 50 nautical miles from the nearest place to get parts and our engine was out of service. Not wanting to tow the *Time out* all the way back to Pender Harbor, we decided that the next day we would take the *Mi-Lil 1* down to Egmont where we had some friends who owned a summer cabin. Our hope was that they'd be home and could drive us to Sechelt to buy a rebuilt carburetor.

Upon arriving at their dock, we were overjoyed to see their car sitting alongside the house. Our friends were kind enough to drive us all the way from Egmont to Sechelt to the nearest auto parts store. Fortunately, we found that the auto parts store had the carburetor we needed in stock. It took most of the day to travel to Sechelt for the carburetor and return back to the boat.

After installing the new carburetor that evening I still had the same problem. Finally, Darrel suggested that I should pull the plugs and check compression, which should have been done in the first place. Sure enough, one cylinder had zero compression. I then removed the valve cover and found that the keepers on one of the exhaust valves had come loose, letting the valve drop down, hitting the piston, and bending the valve stem. We could do nothing to repair the problem so I decided to disable that one cylinder.

We left Princess Louisa Inlet running on only seven cylinders and headed back down Jervis Inlet, into Agamemnon Channel and around into Pender Harbor. It was there that we planned to take moorage at the government dock in Hospital Bay. That worked, but I had to take the idle up to about 800 rpm because anything below that would cause the engine to die. We planned that the *Li-Bre II* and the *Mi-Lil L* would go in ahead of us and try to find a spot on the dock that I could get into without too much maneuvering.

Darrel called on the radio saying he had a spot at the end of the first dock. Perfect, all I had to do was come in and try to judge when to put the boat into neutral and drift on into the spot. I was a few hundred yards from the dock and moving at a pretty good clip, even throwing a bit of a wake. I was embarrassed as Darrel stood at the end of the dock yelling, "Green man at the wheel!" I never saw so many people jump out of their boats at one time. But I was proud of myself. I timed it just right and the boat slid into the dock nice and easy, without any mishaps.

That same summer we returned north to Desolation Sound. We set a time when we and the Haines' could get away for a few weeks together. I had decided to rebuild the engine in our boat before going north that year. However, what we hadn't counted on was the company rebuilding the engine were running behind schedule and the engine wasn't going to be finished in time. Because of this the *Li-Bre II* left ahead of us and we'd get the engine back sometime that week and we'd catch up to them later. Darrel said that he didn't think that would happen and he'd see us when they returned home.

Dorothy and I thought that while we were waiting for the engine, we'd build a new convertible top for the back of the boat. We bought new vinyl material and, using the old top for a pattern, we sewed up a new back cover. After replacing the top and installing the new engine, we decided we could save time getting to Desolation Sound by taking the boat to Campbell River by trailer and leaving from there. Dorothy's place of employment had a branch in Campbell River. They agreed to let us park our truck and boat trailer in their compound for a couple of weeks. As it turned out, the cost was about the same but we did save a day and a half getting there.

After launching the boat in Campbell River, we headed around Cape Mudge on the south end of Quadra Island, past Sutil Point and through Baker Passage. We came past Twin Islands at the lower end of Cortes Island and into the lower end of Homfray Channel. We were then in Desolation Sound Marine Park. We navigated past Mink Island and into Tenedos Bay where we caught up with the *Li-Bri II*. They couldn't believe we not only were able to get the engine installed, but had also built a new top and still caught up with them!

One of our favorite things to do in Tenedos Bay was to

take the dinghy over to the beach where the stream from Unwin Lake empties into the bay. There, you can walk up the trail to the lake and go swimming. On the way, it's a must to stop at one of the many pools in the stream and relax in a nice warm deep pool. It's almost like being in a hot tub.

Then Harold came for another visit. After leaving Tenedos Bay, we came out of Desolation Sound and around into Refuge Cove on the south end of West Redonda Island for fuel and supplies. We headed up Lewis Channel and went into Teakerne Arm on West Redonda Island. We usually anchored in the bay where the waterfall comes down from Cassel Lake. This time, however, there was no room, so we went over to the northwest side of the arm and found an even better place to anchor. We were just off a rocky shore where we could stern tie and pull the back of the boats close enough to step off the swim grids onto a nice big rock that sloped down to the water.

The Haines' daughter, Lisa, who was about 3 or 4 years old at the time, had become attached to me because of an earlier incident: she was running down a wooden dock and got a sliver in her foot. Every time her mother tried to pull it out, she would cry and pull her foot away. I came over and talked to her gently while rubbing her foot. Before she knew it I'd removed the sliver. From that time on she called me Dr. Bobos. I guess Bullis was too hard for her to pronounce.

Back in Teakerne Arm, Lisa and I got off the boats and went for a walk around the shore. When we started back to the boats, we were coming down the rock toward the swim grids to get back aboard, and I slipped on some seaweed. I slid all the way down the barnacle covered rock on my butt, leaving part of my swim suit and a lot of skin on the barnacles! Poor Lisa was crying, "Mr. Bobos, Mr Bobos are you OK?" She was really concerned about me getting hurt.

We managed to gather together enough gauze and bandages between the two boats to get a reasonable patch on my bottom but I couldn't sit comfortably for the next few days. I found that it was more comfortable to wear my swim trunks instead of pants while driving the boat from a standing position. We left Teakerne Arm, going back down Lewis Channel, around Mary Point on Cortes Island, through Baker Passage, around Sutil Point and up into Gorge Harbor on Cortes Island, where we bought some supplies. This time I think we brought on a visit from "Harold" by our own misjudgment.

Instead of going over to the west side of the bay near the marina like most people do, we decided to anchor in the east side. We pulled in and set anchor. I made sure we had a good hold on the bottom. Then the *Li-bre II* rafted to us and we spent the night there. In the morning, when we started to leave, I couldn't get the anchor up. As it turned out, I'd hooked onto a wire cable from the old logging days. We finally took a couple of turns around a rear cleat with the anchor rode, started the engine and pulled. When it came loose, I came up with a dansforth anchor with one flute going up and the other going down. At least I still had an anchor!

We then moved over to the marina and took moorage for the night. We followed the road to the little village of Whaletown, where the ferry comes onto Cortes Island from Quadra Island. On the way, we came across the local farmer's market, and from there we came to the Whaletown post office where we took some pictures. We then looked inside the old church and the Louisa Tooker Library. Next, we went to the old Whaletown general store, situated at the head of the docks and bought ice cream cones.

After a nice night's sleep we left one of the boats at the marina and went aboard the other boat to Manson's Landing and tied up to the public dock. We then hiked up to Hague Lake and enjoyed the day swimming and lying on the beach, soaking up the sun.

One of our favorite spots in Desolation Sound was Melane Cove in Prideaux Haven. That area was so popular that it's a must to tie your stern off to shore. The boats were anchored so close together there was no room to swing on your anchor. We found a spot that looked good to us and set out an anchor. We rafted and then took the dinghy to shore and tied the sterns to a tree. In the afternoon the adults were relaxing in the back of the boats, enjoying the warm afternoon sun while the children took one of the dinghies and went to shore.

Suddenly Darrel looked up and yelled, "Holy cow, look at that!" and pointed toward shore. We saw a mother black bear and her cub walking through the bush just a few feet above where the kids were playing. We called to the kids and pointed to the bears. So what did they do? The boys ran and got into the dinghy and started rowing toward the boats. That left the girls stranded on shore with the bears! The bears just kept walking by and went on their way, not paying any attention to any of us. Darrel took the other dinghy and went to rescue the girls. After that, none of the kids had any desire to go ashore again!

Every time we'd anchor in Prideaux Haven we'd go over to Rosco Bay on West Redonda Island and hike up to Black Lake to go swimming. It was a rather steep trail up to the lake but well worth the hike. The women disliked it because it seemed every time we took the trail to the lake, we came across a couple of snakes.

If you ignore the snakes and didn't mind the steep hike, it's a beautiful lake to enjoy. There were big flat rocks at the water's edge where you could enjoy the sun or jump into the nice clear water of the lake. This seemed to be one place where "Harold" never went. Every time we've gone to Black Lake we've never had a visit from the little black cloud.

We did have one enjoyable time without a visit from Harold. On one of our trips north, we made a stop in Campbell River and tried bucktail fishing for Coho Salmon. This was the most exciting type of fishing we'd ever experienced.

We had a friend named Fred who was working part time as a fishing guide in the area. Fred promised that if we were ever in Campbell River during the Coho Salmon run to give him a call, he would take us out and show us how to go bucktailing. We arrived in Campbell River on a Friday afternoon and called Fred. Unfortunately he had a client to take out the next day but said he'd come down to the boat that afternoon and give us some advice. He took us up to the local tackle shop and told us what to buy to go bucktailing. He then went back to the boat with us and showed us how to rig our lines. After getting our gear ready, Fred proceeded to tell us where to go for the best fishing. He told us to troll along the west side of Quadra Island between Quathiaski Cove and Cape Mudge. Fred said the trick was to troll at a speed fast enough to create a small wake behind the boat. Then we were to let out enough line so the bucktail fly was trailing just before the wake.

The next morning we got up early and headed across Johnstone Strait to the fishing grounds. We found we were not the only ones out hoping to catch a Coho, there must have been 25 or more boats out. They were all trolling rapidly against the current. We made our way into the line of boats, set our speed and put out our lines. We were moving along at a pretty good pace with the other boats around us doing the same. Suddenly, Dorothy's reel started to sing from a salmon on the line. I had to maneuver the boat out of the line of traffic so we could put the engine in neutral and land the fish. I fought the traffic from the other boats while Dorothy did her best to keep the fish from getting loose. Then my reel started singing from a salmon on my pole. I had difficulties trying to run the boat while keeping my line from getting tangled with Dorothy's or with the other fishermen's. We finally managed to get clear of other boats, but in the process, the fish on my line got loose. However, we did manage to get Dorothy's fish on board.

We fished for a little over an hour. Two other times we both had fish on our lines at the same time. We lost more fish than we landed, but we did get our limit.

We then realized we had more salmon than we could handle because we were on our way north in a boat that couldn't freeze the fish. All we had aboard was a small ice box. Earlier, we'd been talking on the radio to our friend Dave who was aboard the *Salute*. He was mooching off Cape Mudge and wasn't having much luck. That gave me an idea. We headed for Cape Mudge and found the *Salute.* I pulled alongside and asked Dave to show me his salmon net. When he held it over the side of his boat, I reached over and dropped two salmon into his net. "Now you can't say you haven't caught anything", I said. We turned our boat and headed north as we waved good by to the *Salute*.

CHAPTER EIGHT:

Rough Water, Fog and Outboards

Upon joining the Cruising Club, we did a lot more family cruising with other boaters. The club always planned a cruise every holiday weekend. We went to places like Plumper Cove on Keats Island, across the Strait of Georgia to Telegraph Harbor Marina on Thetis Island, Newcastle Island by Nanaimo and over to what then was called Manianna Lodge in Ladysmith Harbor.

On one of these trips, we spent the weekend at Telegraph Harbor Marina. We had a great weekend and the weather was perfect. When it came time to leave, some boaters decided to stay and continue cruising in the Gulf Islands, but we had to head for home.

We struck out on our own, going through the passage between Thetis Island and Kuper Island, through Porlier Pass and on across the Strait of Georgia, heading for home. Leaving Porlier Pass, the sea conditions were good. Only light winds with one and a half foot seas with a slight chop. We set a course for Vancouver Harbor.

What we didn't know was the little black cloud was following us. We were half way across when the wind picked up and the seas got rougher. We thought we'd be all right and instead of turning back, we kept on going toward Vancouver.

Suddenly, we discovered the wind had blown us into the shallow water off the Sand Heads west of the Vancouver Airport. Because of the shallow water, we were in waves close to eight feet high. I cut back on our speed because we were heading into seas so big that when we came down into the trough between seas, we could see nothing but water all around us. We tried to pull out into deeper water but were afraid to get the waves on our beam and cause us to capsize. When we were down in the trough, I had to lay my head on the dash to see the top of the next wave as it came toward us. Dorothy took a rope and tied it around our waists, then tied it to the boat. She said if we got swamped, we would stay with the boat.

The boat was being tossed around so much, all the cupboards came open. Things were flying all over. The table come off its hooks and was lying on the floor. I was sure a couple of times the gunnels of the boat were under water. In those days we didn't have a VHF radio, but we did have a CB radio and there was a fellow CB operator living in the Point Grey area monitoring channel nine. We radioed him and told him that we were having difficulty but were doing okay at this time. He said he'd keep in contact and, if we needed the Coast Guard, he would call them for us.

About that time, a fishing trawler in the 50 foot range

passed us. We thought that if we got in behind him, maybe he could break a path for us. That didn't work because every time his bow went down into a wave, his propellers came out of the water and sprayed us with sea water! In the meantime, the fellow on the CB radio kept calling us to see how we were doing. That gave us some comfort.

We fought our way through those seas for about an hour before finally coming to the mouth of the north arm of the Fraser River. We were now in deeper water and smoother seas, so we could make our way around Point Grey and head home. We learned a couple of things from that trip: one was our boat could take a lot rougher seas that we had thought, and two, that when we are crossing a large body of water, we needed to watch the wind and current, keeping track of how much we were being blown off course.

We spent many weekends on the boat just to be out on the water or sometimes, to do some fishing. Once we spent the weekend in the Gibsons area, came back through the First Narrows, and were going home. There was a good wind blowing most of the day and, when a strong wind blows against the outgoing tide through the first narrows, there are usually a few standing waves just before going under the bridge.

We not only had standing waves to deal with, but there was also a tug boat coming out of the harbor at the same time. Our daughter was asleep in the forward bunk. I had closed the hatch on the forward deck but neglected to lock it. I cut our speed down trying not to take the waves too hard, but the waves from the tug boat had combined with the standing waves. The bow went over the first wave, came down and went through the second one. When the bow came down, the hatch flew open. When we went through the next wave about two or three gallons of water come through the open hatch, falling straight down on our daughter. She woke up, thinking the boat was sinking. She came flying out of the bunk, through the cabin and was ready to jump overboard. She would have made it if I hadn't reached out and grabbed her as she went by the helm station.

On Easter weekend 1975, Harold hit us all. The Cruising Club cruised to Plumper Cove on Keats Island. The weather was good, and we served a pancake breakfast one morning on shore so everyone was enjoying themselves. Some members went fishing and came back with some nice sized salmon. Most of us spent the time just sitting around the docks enjoying each other's company.

On Sunday evening, we all went to our boats for a good nights' sleep. At daylight on Monday morning, I was awakened by people yelling and running around the dock. Someone banged on the side of our boat, telling us we'd have to get up and get out. We were moored on the inside, next to one of our members who had a 36 foot heavy wooden boat, so we couldn't see what was happening. When I came out, I was nearly blown into the water. A storm came up and there were near hurricane force winds blowing in from the south. We were experiencing two foot waves rolling into the docks at Plumper Cove. All the boats were being tossed around against the docks and straining on their mooring lines.

It was decided that we had to get away and move somewhere more protected from the wind. We headed for Center Bay on Gambier Island, hoping we would be more out of the wind. By the time we left Plumper Cove we were in seas equal to that in the Strait of Georgia. It was difficult even getting away from the docks, without being blown back against them.

Coming across the channel to Gambier was very difficult. We were in following seas and actually being pushed across by the wind. We made it into Center Bay and tucked ourselves behind Alexander Island. We rafted and set out three anchors, which held us in place for the rest of the day. It was exciting sitting there listening to the wind and trying to keep our canvas side curtains from being blown away. By late afternoon, the wind died down and we were able to head home. During the next week we discovered how fortunate we'd been to have avoided any serious damage. We'd heard and read stories about boats being blown off anchors and away from docks. Some boats had been totally destroyed.

Fog was always a problem in the fall and winter. Once,

when we were coming home from an outing, we headed for False Creek and encountered a thick fog bank just off the end of Stanley Park. Before we went into the fog, I took a compass bearing on the entrance to False Creek. When moving along at a slow idle speed and looking forward, it always seems like you are going in circles. It's hard to trust your compass. Dorothy kept telling me we were going the wrong way but I stayed on the compass course. The next thing we saw was the Kitsilano Coast Guard station. That was a good feeling.

On one clear winter day, we went to meet the *Li-Bre II* in Snug Cove on Bowen Island. Coming out of the harbor heading toward Point Atkinson, we encountered a fog bank across the entrance to Howe Sound and extending out into the Strait. The *Li-Bre II* was exiting Fishermans Cove. We called them on the radio to see how they were doing. Darrel answered saying that if he stayed close to shore, he could get around Point Atkinson and meet us. However the fog would be really bad going over to Bowen Island.

Then our friend Dave called us from aboard the *Salute*. He was trolling in the fog fishing off the Point Grey bell buoy and had heard us on the radio. Because Dave does a lot of log racing with the *Salute* and knows his boat speed at any RPM, he said he could get us through the fog. We met off Point Atkinson and got in a line behind the *Salute* heading into the fog bank. When we left Point Atkinson, Dave said we could be at the entrance to Snug Cove in 22 minutes. The fog was so thick I had to stay within three boat lengths to see Darrel's boat in front of me. We moved along at a slow speed, talking back and forth on the radios. Suddenly Dave yelled for everyone to reverse and stop immediately. We came to a halt wondering what the problem was. I looked up and saw this big white monster coming out of the fog going right across our path. There went one of the BC ferries headed for Horseshoe Bay.

We stopped until the ferry was gone. Then Dave announced that we'd taken a five minute timeout and now we would arrive in 27 minutes. We continued on to Snug Cove. I then looked over and saw the light marking the entrance to the cove. We were off our time by nearly three minutes. That showed the advantage of knowing your exact boat speed at all times. We were also glad Harold wasn't around at the time. After the fog lifted we had a great time enjoying a nice, cold winters day with other boating friends. We had no trouble getting back home.

Another time some of the Cruising Club boats went over to the Gibsons public dock for the weekend. On the way home we ran into fog in Queen Charlotte Channel alongside Bowen Island. We pulled into Deep Bay on the east side of Bowen Island and dropped anchor. We hoped the fog would soon lift enough for us to get on home. After sitting there for a few hours, it started getting dark. One of the boats had an older model radar on board but the owner didn't know how reliable it was. We agreed we would give it a try.

We were concerned about ship traffic coming out through the first narrows. After going around Point Atkinson, we headed for the Narrows. We called Traffic Control on channel twelve on the VHF radio. They said all was clear and that they could see us on their radar. They said we looked like a mother duck and her ducklings going along the North Shore. They also told us that once we were past the entrance to First Narrows, we would be out of the fog. It's nice to know that Vancouver Traffic is there willing to assist boaters when needed. We all made it home safe and before dark.

The worst time I had in the fog was the time my boating friend, Dick asked me to help bring his boat, the *Candida,* from his mooring in Coal Harbor through the harbor and to the Port Moody launch ramp. He was going to have the *Candida* hauled home for the winter and do some work on her.

We were headed up the inner harbor and doing well until we got to the Second Narrows bridge. There we encountered a thick fog bank sitting just on the other side of the bridge. I was at the helm so I slowed down and told Dick to get out his chart of the inner harbor. I wanted to work out a compass course to get us to Port Moody. Dick looked at me strangely and said, "I don't have any charts on board, I took everything off the boat knowing I was bringing it home for the season". I figured it was a pretty straight run from the bridge to

Port Moody. All I had to do was look out for Berry Point and Gosse Point. I took a compass bearing just before going into the fog and put Dick up on the bow, telling him to look for the shore on our starboard side. We slowly made our way through the fog favoring the starboard side. Whenever we came close to shore, Dick would signal me and I'd move over to port a bit.

When we were about where I thought we'd start making a turn to the starboard and try to find the entrance to the Port Moody boat launch ramp, Dick came back to the helm and told me to shut off the engine. I complied. Dick told me to listen. He thought he had heard someone calling. We listened and, sure enough, we heard a small voice yelling for help.

Dick went back up on the bow and directed me toward the call. It wasn't long before we came across a young boy around eleven years old, standing on a five foot square floating platform, which was anchored in the middle of the flats at the end of the inlet. The fog was so thick that we almost ran into the float before seeing it. The poor boy was so cold and scared he could hardly speak. He told us that before the fog, some of his friends had taken him out in their boat, put him on the float and then couldn't find him after the fog set in. I remembered seeing that float before so I knew it was almost straight out from the Port Moody launch ramp. I turned the boat 90 degrees starboard and headed toward the ramp. Upon arriving there, we were surprised to find the boat mover still waiting for us. As soon as the boat was close to the dock, the boy jumped off and was running for home before we could even offer him a ride.

We've also had some trouble with the little black cloud when it came to outboard motors. It seems we kept dumping them in the salt chuck. Once we were rafted with the *Li-Bre II* in Bedwell Bay up Indian Arm. The kids were out playing around in the dinghies. We were having a relaxing afternoon in the boats enjoying the warm afternoon sun. Then Darrel looked up and saw his son coming back toward the boat, swinging his outboard motor back and forth making the dinghy zig zag. Suddenly, the motor came off the dinghy and went overboard!

We were anchored in about 40 feet of water on a flood tide. None of us were really good swimmers so diving for the motor was out of the question. We tried dragging hooks for it but with no success. We finally gave up and went home, thinking the motor was lost. The next day, however, Darrel found someone who went back with him to dive for the motor. They found the outboard motor and he took it home. After cleaning it immediately with fresh water, Darrel pulled off the carburetor and cleaned it with fresh gasoline. After a few pulls, the motor started. Darrel used that motor for several more years!

In the summer of '77, we headed south to the San Juan Islands and stopped at Telegraph Harbor for a couple of days on the way.

Our son and another friend's son had taken their dinghies out for a spin. Then I saw the two boys coming back toward the marina, both of them in our friend's dinghy, while pulling our dinghy which was upside down. All I could see was the bow of the dinghy and the shaft of the motor with the propeller sticking out of the water.

As it turned out, the boys had gone over by the ferry landing to a youth camp. Being true boys, they ran around doing donuts in the water and showing off for the girls. Then our son lost control of his boat and flipped it over.

Again, we lifted the motor onto the dock, pulled out the spark plugs and removed the carburetor. We cleaned everything with fresh water and put some oil into the cylinders. Within an hour we had the motor running again. We kept that outboard motor for another ten years before selling it. As far as we know it's still running!

That little black cloud Harold has a habit of moving around on other boating friends too. One evening we stopped for coffee with the Haines. Darrel received a phone call from one of our fellow boaters. This was our friend Dave, who owned the 36 foot wooden cruiser the *Salute*. As mentioned, he often used the *Salute* for log racing. This meant it was necessary to know exactly what the boat speed was at different RPMs.

Dave and his wife had been out that afternoon doing speed runs off the Point Grey mile marker. Not watching where he was going, he hit a dead head off Wreck Beach, and put a hole in the bow. They tried putting life jackets and cushions in the hole but found the bilge pumps were unable to keep up with the incoming water. It was an ebb tide, so they decided that to save the boat, the best thing to do was to run it onto the beach. The nearest beach was Wreck Beach where clothing is optional. Giving the boat full throttle ahead and as the bow got lower in the water, Dave ran the boat aground. The propellers hit the rocks and finally stalled the engines. He told us he didn't realize until later that the person he had tossed the bow line to wasn't wearing any clothes!

When the tide went out and he knew the boat was going to stay put, Dave crawled up the bank and phoned Darrel for help. Darrel, another boater, and I, gathered some plywood, assorted screws and as many tubes of calking as we could find and headed for U B C to make our way to the boat. It took us a couple of hours to get the plywood attached over the hole. By this time, it was after midnight, and the tide was starting to come in. We figured that in three hours the water would be high enough to put the boat afloat, so we could pull it off the beach.

We left the skipper aboard and took his wife home.

We then went home ourselves to get a couple of hours sleep. We would come back the next morning with another boat to pull the *Salute* off the beach.

At around seven the next morning we arrived by water to find the *Salute* sitting at anchor with plenty of water under her. We took her in tow and pulled her over to Fisherman's Cove, where they put her on land. Dave told us the patch was holding so well that after the boat was afloat, during the tow to Fisherman's Cove, the bilge pump very seldom came on.

As a teenager living in Oregon, I learned to sail on the Columbia River.

A friend of the family had a beautiful wooden sloop. It was about 30feet long and had a low mahogany cabin which the owner kept varnished and in perfect condition.

He loved sailing on the river and was out on the water whenever time would allow. His wife didn't like sailing and very seldom went with him. However, she always worried about him when he went sailing by himself. She was concerned he'd fall overboard with no one to assist him. Therefore, he was always looking for a sailing partner. He knew that I loved being on the water, so he asked my parents if he could take me with him and teach me how to sail. My parents said "Okay"! I jumped at the chance to go sailing and spent a lot of time over the next two summers sailing on that beautiful wooden sloop.

After moving to British Columbia, the owner of the company I worked for decided he wanted to buy a sailboat. He'd never owned a boat before so he asked me if I knew anything about sailboats. I explained to him about the limited sailing experience I'd had and told him that I'd assist him as much as possible. I neglected to tell him about my friend Harold.

He was looking at a 26-foot Thunderbird sloop listed for sale through a broker in West Vancouver. We made arrangements with the salesman one weekend to take the boat out for a sea trial. My boss, his wife, the salesman and I took the boat out of the marina into the waters of Howe Sound. We hoisted the sails while there was a light breeze blowing and headed past Point Atkinson toward Point Grey. All was going well as we enjoyed the sail on the beautiful sunny day. Suddenly the wind started coming in short, strong gusts. I looked out into the Strait of Georgia and saw a grey cloud with long streaks reaching down to the water, coming our way. I knew right away it was a squall heading toward us. Before we could get turned around to head back to the marina, the squall hit us. Suddenly we found ourselves in winds gusting to 25 knots and it was pouring down rain. My boss started panicking and yelled,

"Oh my, oh my, what do we do now?"

"We need to get some of this sail down", I said.

I turned the tiller over to the salesman and told him to keep the boat headed into the wind as much as possible. I then went forward and lowered the jib. After getting the jib down, I went back and reefed the main sail to reduce the size of the sail. By that time the squall had passed and everything started calming down. We unfurled the main, raised the jib again and headed back to the marina. That experience proved to my boss that he could make a lot of mistakes sailing that little boat and still come out okay, so he bought it.

A few months later, Harold came aboard again. My boss and his wife invited Dorothy and me out for an afternoon sail. It was a great day for sailing. A gentle wind was blowing through Howe Sound. We were enjoying a long reach, heading up Queen Charlotte Channel.

I was at the helm when suddenly I discovered I had the tiller in my hand but it wasn't attached to anything! Upon further investigation, I found that the collar on the shaft holding the rudder in place had come loose and the rudder had fallen overboard. Now what do we do? We had no steerage.

If you are familiar with the Thunderbird sailboat, you know they're equipped with an outboard motor setting in a well in the back of the boat. The motor sets in the well so tight that it won't turn to steer the boat. It would be impossible to sail this boat against the wind without steerage. We could use the motor for propulsion but had no way to turn the boat.

Then I got an idea. The cabin door consisted of three plywood boards set down into slots to close off the cabin from the cockpit. I started the outboard and, going at a very slow speed, we took two of the boards from the cabin door and each of us got on the two sides of the boat. We dragged the board in the water on the side we wanted to turn. The boat then made a slow turn in that direction. By doing this we made our way back to the marina and into our slip.

CHAPTER NINE:

Beyond Desolation Sound

The last trip we took north in the *Time Out* was in the summer of 1978. We decided to go further north than Desolation Sound. We'd been told how beautiful the scenery was and about all the wildlife we'd see when we got to places like the Octopus Islands, Owen Bay, Big Bay, Shoal Bay and Blind Channel. We'd also been told how good the fishing was up there. We were a little apprehensive because of all the rapids, including The Yacultus, Hole in the Wall, Arran, Dents and the Green Point rapids. We talked to some boaters who said they wouldn't even consider going into that area because of the rapids.

After considerable discussion with the Haines', we concluded that with our faster boats and high horsepower engines, we wouldn't have any problems negotiating the rapids. We'd just watch our tide and current tables and pick the proper times to navigate through the rapids. However, we were a little concerned about going into those areas with the possibility of the little black cloud following us.

After spending a night in Rebecca Spit Marine Park, we then headed to Heriot Bay on Quadra Island for gas and supplies. After leaving Heriot Bay, our first challenge was going through Surge Narrows on our way to The Octopus Islands. We picked a time to leave Heriot Bay and started out into Hoskyn Channel towards Surge Narrows.

We went through Surge Narrows on the tail end of an ebb tide and got through with no problem. Then, just outside of Surge Narrows, we made our first wildlife sighting. I saw something in the water ahead of us and, upon closer look, discovered it was a grey whale coming toward us. We could see it come to the surface sporadically and then disappear again. I stopped the boat and waited to see where the whale was headed. It came within about a quarter mile of us and then submerged. We never saw it again.

After a couple days exploring the Octopus Islands, Harold returned. We were getting ready to go to bed when I smelled gasoline. I looked into the engine compartment but couldn't see any fuel leaking around the engine. Upon further exploration, I discovered that we had a very small leak in the port fuel tank. .

The *Time Out* had two 60 gallon fuel tanks, one on each side of the boat. They sat on the floor under the side decks. I checked the fuel gauge and found we had less than a quarter tank of fuel left in the port tank. I used up the remaining fuel in that tank so I could switch over and run on the starboard tank only. That cut my fuel capacity in half, but thought we'd still be able to make it between fuel stops.

We left the Octopus Islands at a time when we could go through the Hole in the Wall without fighting too large of a current. We headed for Big Bay on Stuart Island. We made it through the Hole in the Wall with no problems. By the time we arrived in Big Bay, it was getting late in the evening and the dock was full. We had no place to stay. The dock master told us he thought the current was still slack enough to get through Gillard Pass and the Dent Rapids. He said there was good anchorage in Mermaid Bay on Dent Island, commonly known as Tugboat Haven because that was where the tugboats sat waiting for slack tide before coming through the Dents and the Yuculta Rapids.

We anchored in Tugboat Haven for the night. We were intrigued by all the pieces of wood with boat names on them nailed to the trees. These had been left by the boats anchored in the bay before us. Almost every tree along the shore had several names posted on it. We decided not to add our names to the bunch as it was getting dark and we hadn't had our dinner.

After dinner we sat in the *LI-Bre II,* listening to the chatter on the VHF radio when we picked up a conversation between two fishing vessels. As near as we could tell by their conversation, they were heading south down Cordero Channel and were about to enter the Dent Rapids. They were talking about their fishing experience. They thought they'd get through the rapids without any trouble because they were going with the current.

Then one said, “What do you think George?”

There was no answer and he kept calling, “George, George are you there?”

There was a long pause and finally George came back and said, “Yeah I’m here, I just hit a whirlpool and when the boat rolled over, I was knocked off my stool”!

Then they went on with their conversation as if nothing had happened!

Later that evening we decided to figure out what time slack tide would be in the morning. That way we could get back through the Dent Rapids and into Big Bay. Darrel took the tide and current book and sat down to figure it out. After some time he said we should be ready to go at 9:45 AM. That would put us through at slack.

The next morning, after breakfast, we pulled anchor and headed for Big Bay just before 9:45 AM. We headed into Cordeo Channel, down through the Dent Rapids, through Gillard Pass and into Big Bay. To me it looked like the current was running too fast to be slack tide. I thought maybe we were just a little ahead of time, so we kept going. By the time we were at the top of the Dent Rapids I knew something was wrong. There was white water and whirlpools all over the place. By then we were committed, so we kept going. About halfway through the rapids, I looked over the side of the boat. What I saw put a real scare into me. There was a large whirlpool opening up right alongside the boat! Reaching down, I pushed the throttle to full speed, just as the boat was about to be pulled into the whirlpool. Luckily we had enough power to keep ourselves out of trouble.

Coming out of Gillard Pass into Big Bay, we headed toward the marina. The current was running so strong we found ourselves halfway through Big Bay and almost into the Yucultas before making any headway toward shore. Finally we got back to the marina and tied up. I went over to the *Li-Bre II* and asked Darrel to check his calculations again. After a little while he came back and said,

"Guess what, I was wrong. I had it backwards. We came through at maximum run, not slack."

From that time on, whenever we calculated tides and currents, we worked it out together.

As we came into Big Bay, we noticed a large boat moored to the end of the dock. It was grey and looked like an ex-navy boat of some type. Upon closer inspection, we saw the name on the boat was *The Grey Goose*. I told Darrel that I thought *The Grey Goose* was a converted World War II sub-chaser and belonged to John Wayne. As we walked up the dock toward the store, we passed a big fellow wearing a red plaid shirt. Sure enough, there went John Wayne!

From Big Bay on Stuart Island, we went up Cordero Channel, past Frederick Arm, stopping at Shoal Bay across from Phillips Arm for fuel because of my lower capacity.

Upon arriving at Shoal Bay, we found the fuel dock was closed. This meant the next fuel stop was Blind Channel Resort on the north end of East Thurlow Island. We decided if I ran out of fuel, all we could do was have Darrel take us in tow.

We headed on down Cordero Channel. Just as we approached the head of Mayne Passage, my engine ran out of fuel. We were prepared though and had the tow ropes ready to go. Soon Darrel had us in tow and headed toward the fuel dock at Blind Channel Resort.

We enjoyed the sights and hiked up a trail to a giant 80-year-old cedar tree. We went to bed that night hoping to do more sightseeing the next day. Then Harold struck again. I got up the next morning, walked out onto the back deck and stepped into a pool of gasoline on the floor. Looking closer I discovered that the starboard fuel tank had developed a leak.

When you're in the middle of nowhere, you do the best you can. I always keep some type of repair product on the boat. After rummaging around, I found some two part epoxy repair. We first cleaned up the gasoline on the floor, pulled the boat apart right there at the dock, and removed the first tank that had leaked while in the Octopus Islands. We set it out in the sun to dry and patched the leak with the epoxy. After letting the epoxy cure for most of the day, we reinstalled the tank. Darrel's boat had a twelve volt electric fuel pump feeding fuel to the carburetor. We removed the pump from his boat, did a temporary hook up on my boat to transfer the fuel from the leaking tank over to the repaired tank, and went on our way.

CHAPTER TEN:

New Boat New Experiences

In the early 1980s we sold the *Time Out* and bought a 32-foot wooden boat built in Vancouver in 1957. It was named *The Alahanna,* pronounced Alanna, Gaelic for "my little one". We restored and rebuilt it, changing it from a single cabin express cruiser to a double cabin command bridge cruiser. We also replaced the twin V-drive Chrysler Hemi gas engines with direct drive four cylinder Perkins diesel engines.

When we rebuilt *The Alahanna,* we did so with the thought of doing some long range cruising. She carried 120 gallons of fuel which, with her twin four cylinder diesel engines, gave her a cruising range of around 250 nautical miles. She was also fitted with a fifty gallon fresh water tank. In the head there was a full stand alone shower. To get hot water for the shower and the galley, we installed a propane instant fired hot water heater. The galley was equipped with a three burner propane stove with an oven as well as a microwave oven. For refrigeration, there was a six cubic foot refrigerator/freezer combination operating on shore power or propane. The electrical system consisted of twelve volt and 110 volt shore power. She carried four six-volt golf cart batteries for the house system and two twelve volt batteries for engine start. She had a 1000 watt power inverter that would convert 12 volts DC to 120 volts AC and a 1500 watt generator to operate the microwave oven and other small appliances while at anchor. For heating in cold weather, she was equipped with a diesel fired wall heater. When under way, a hot water heater ran off the starboard engine.

About the time we sold the *Time Out,* the Haines' sold the LiBri II and bought a 25-foot Sangster Craft named the Nancy G. We were then rebuilding the Alahanna. This took a few years and we were missing being on the water. Darrel offered to let us use his boat for a weekend. We weren't about to turn down a chance to go cruising. What we didn't think about was that little black cloud, Harold. The Nancy G was moored at Thunderbird Marina in West Vancouver. Dorothy and I decided that a good weekend cruise would be to go from Thunderbird Marina to Keats Island across from Gibsons.

It was spring time and Darrel said it might take a while to get the engine started because he hadn't used the boat for some time. We arrived at the marina and loaded all our gear aboard. I should have known this was a perfect time for Harold to visit. I tried starting the engine. It took several tries but it finally started. At first it ran roughly but as it warmed up, it started to smooth out. I thought the problem was just moisture in the engine from sitting for so long. By the time the engine got up to the right temperature, it was running well so we left the marina. As we got out into open water, I increased our speed. The engine was misfiring quite badly but I hoped it would eventually warm up and smooth out. We headed up Howe Sound and started around the top of Bowen Island. The engine was still running rough and I couldn't get the boat up to speed. I finally decided I was going to have to find the cause of problem. I turned off the engine and, while sitting adrift, I discovered that three of the eight cylinders weren't firing. I traced the problem to be the distributor cap. All the contract points were corroded, three of them very badly.

I knew Darrel would have a drawer or storage area aboard with spare parts. I rummaged around in the boat and finally found the spare parts bin with two extra distributor caps. I took one of the caps and transferred all the sparkplug lead wires to it. When I tried putting the new cap on the distributor, I found that it didn't fit. I got the other cap and moved all the wires onto that cap only to find that it didn't fit the distributor either. Darrel had some sandpaper and emery cloth aboard so I took the emery cloth and cleaned the contacts in the original cap as well as I could. After installing the cap, I turned the key and the engine started immediately. We headed on to Keats Island and enjoyed the rest of the weekend.

Upon telling Darrel the problem we had, he informed us that last year, he had installed a new engine in the boat and those caps were for the old engine. He hadn't thought about getting new caps for the new engine.

M.V. Alahanna

About the same time we launched *The Alahanna,* the Haines' bought a 28-Foot wooden Trojan power boat. Their new boat was named the *Marizion*. We kept the boats at Reed Point Marina in Port Moody and spent a lot of time cruising up Indian Arm and anchoring overnight in Bedwell Bay.

Marazion

Harold followed us onto the new boats as well. It was only our first or second time out in the *Alahanna* when we were on our way back from a weekend in Howe Sound. We came around Point Atkinson and headed into the harbor. The weather was sunny and warm without a breath of wind. The seas were flat calm. We were running the boat from the command bridge and, perhaps because of the beautiful weather, I wasn't as alert as I should have been.

Suddenly I looked down in front of the boat and saw a piece of driftwood about eight or ten inches long headed under the bow. It was too late to steer around it. The wood went directly under the boat and we heard it thump against the bottom. I pulled back on the throttles and knocked it out of gear, but not soon enough. The chunk of wood hit the starboard prop. When I put the engines back into gear and started off again, there was a horrible vibration throughout the boat. After shutting down the starboard engine, we made our way back to Reed Point Marina, running on the port engine only.

Later that week, I contacted a friend who had diving gear. He came down to the marina, dove under the boat and removed the propeller. He came up with a propeller with one blade only half there and another badly bent.

After getting the propeller repaired, my diving friend came back and reinstalled it. He wouldn't accept payment for his efforts but asked if I'd take him and another diving buddy up Indian Arm for a day of diving.

A couple of weeks later Dorothy and I took them for a day of diving off Croker Island at the head of Indian Arm.

After buying a wooden boat, we decided to join the Vancouver Wooden Boat Society. We made a lot of new friends and enjoyed the company of fellow wooden boat owners through the Society. We entered *The Alahanna* in several of the annual Wooden Boat Festivals on Granville Island. At one of them we were voted first place for Best Restoration.

On one of the first outings with the Vancouver Wooden Boat Society, Harold returned. The club sponsored a cruise to Halkett Bay on Gambier Island in Howe Sound. We set anchors and rafted out in the bay. In the afternoon, a wind blew down into the bay from the north. Our anchors couldn't hold us against the wind so we began drifting out of the bay. We decided to pull the anchors and move to one of the log rafts and tie up for the night.

As luck would have it, in the middle of the night we were awakened by a tug boat. The crew told us to get off the raft because they were taking it away. We untied from the raft and drifted around in the bay until the tug boat headed out of the bay with the raft. We came back to the log raft and prepared to tie up for the rest of the night.

Because there was a large space between two rafts,

Dorothy and I decided to tie in this space between the rafts instead of tying on the outside. We were getting ready to get back in bed when Dorothy noticed the raft north of us was getting close and closing the gap at a fast pace. I started the engines and sent Dorothy forward to release the bow line. I went out back to release the lines from the stern. When I got there, I looked over the side and saw that the north raft was only about three feet from the side of the boat. I called for Dorothy to take the line off the cleat and let it go while I did the same. I ran into the cabin, threw the boat into gear and hit the throttles.

We pulled away from the log rafts just as they were coming together. Luckily, we escaped with just a small scratch on the side in the stern. Another minute or two more and we'd have been crushed between the log booms as they drifted together!

Not long afterward I took a friend from work out for a weekend fishing trip. We decided to try our luck around the Gibsons area. Leaving the marina around mid morning, we started trolling along the end of Bowen Island. It was a terrible day! The rain came down in sheets and it was very windy. Hence, the seas were quite rough. Because of the bad weather we didn't get to do much fishing that afternoon. We finally gave up and decided to go into Plumper Cove and anchor for the night, hoping that the next day would be better. The wind and rain continued for most of the night.

By early morning, the wind had died down, but it still rained on and off. We got up and motored into Gibsons Gap where we lowered our downriggers, trolling around the south end of Barfleur Passage and on out into Georgia Strait. The seas were much calmer but there was still a good ground swell rolling in from the previous day's storm.

My friend was out tending to the fishing lines. I was at the helm trying to keep the boat on course. Suddenly, we got a visit from Harold. The boat was drifting to starboard, so I gave the wheel a turn to port. I couldn't feel any resistance on the wheel. The rudder wasn't responding! Immediately, I put the boat into neutral and we pulled in the fishing gear. I then discovered we had a broken hydraulic steering line. We were only a short distance from Gibsons, so we tried to make it into the government dock to find the parts needed to repair the hydraulic line. This is where twin engines come in handy. I maneuvered the boat into Gibsons and up to the dock by using the throttles and shifting the engines in and out of gear.

As we were getting secured to the dock, a hard rain returned. Without rain gear or an umbrella, we headed to town to find the parts we needed. Then we discovered that there were no hardware stores or auto parts stores in lower Gibsons. The nearest parts supplier was up the hill in the newer part of town. If you've ever been in Gibsons you'd know that it's quite a distance up that hill to where we needed to go.

Because of the rain, the fact that we were getting soaked and didn't know what the bus schedule was like, we decided to take a taxi to the store. We found the couplers needed to make the repair. Then, being a little short on cash and the rain having stopped, we decided to walk back to the boat. We were about half way down the hill when it started raining again.

Once back to the boat, the first thing I did was start the diesel heater to get us dry. After drying out, I went down into the engine compartment and made the repair. I added more hydraulic fluid, bled the air out of the system and we were ready to go. By that time, most of the day was gone so we headed for home. After all that and having not caught any fish, my friend never did ask to go fishing with me again!

One weekend, when Dorothy's brother and sister-in-law were visiting, we decided to take them out in the boat for the day. We headed for Deep Cove in Indian Arm. Our plan was to take moorage at the government dock and walk uptown. We arrived to find the government dock full, so we decided to anchor in the bay north of the Deep Cove Yacht Club.

After setting the anchor in about 50 feet of water and making sure we had a good hold, we put the dinghy down, rowed over to the government dock and headed for town. We walked around for about an hour and stopped to have ice cream cones before heading back to the dinghy.

We were walking toward the dock when I looked toward the north shore of the cove. I commented to Dorothy that there was a boat tied to a dock across the bay that looked very similar to ours. As we got closer, I realized that it not only looked like our boat; it was our boat! Dorothy and I immediately ran for the dinghy and left our relatives standing on the dock. We jumped into the dinghy and headed for our boat.

We discovered that the dock belonged to a boating acquaintance of ours who lived on the north shore of Deep Cove. He said that our boat would drift for a bit before the anchor would catch, hold for a while, then lose ground and set the boat adrift again. Thinking he recognized the boat, he sent his son out in their outboard motor boat to bring it into their dock before it drifted out into the open water.

He told us we'd just discovered why it's called Deep Cove. We'd set our anchor on the edge of the shelf in the cove where if dropped from about 50 feet to over 100 feet within a span of less than 50 yards. In the afternoon a breeze came up, pulled our anchor off the shelf and set the boat adrift. We thanked our acquaintance for retrieving our boat, and motored back to the government dock to pick up our relatives.

One warm Saturday, we called some friends and asked if they'd like to go for a boating trip up Indian Arm. They accepted our invitation and we all met at the marina. We boarded *The Alahanna* and headed out for a boat ride. On the way up Indian Arm we stopped and put out a couple of crab traps. We then traveled up Indian Arm and enjoyed the sunshine. We took a run around the Twin Islands and stopped to drift just off the north shore and have lunch. After lunch we went back and checked the crab traps. Then we thought we would go and drop anchor in the little cove behind Admiralty point. We could row the dinghy over to Maple Beach and from there, we could walk to Belcarra Park.

After getting the anchor set, we put the dinghy down, put the two ladies in the dinghy and I rowed them over to the beach. I then went back to the boat to get the last crew member. He was big, stood over six feet tall and weighed well over 200 pounds. I put him in the rear seat of the dinghy and rowed toward shore. We were a bit heavy in the back to say the least! When the bow of the dinghy ran on to the beach, the waves from a passing boat hit us from behind and totally swamped us. We were both soaked from the waist down! It was a warm day though, so by the time we'd walked to Belcarra Park and back, we were quite dry. Upon returning to the beach, I made sure there were no boats going by before getting back into the dinghy.

CHAPTER ELEVEN:

Harold in the Gulf Islands

On one of our first trips in *The Alahanna,* we went to the Gulf Islands where we were accompanied by Harold once more. We'd had a comfortable trip crossing the Strait of Georgia and were making our way into Silva Bay. Upon finding Silva Bay way too crowded with no place for comfortable anchorage, we navigated our way through Gabriola Passage and pulled into Degnen Bay on the southwest side of Gabriola Island. We were about to drop anchor in the bay when we saw a boat leaving from the government dock.

That was when Harold struck us. We turned and headed for the dock and were only a few yards out when I pulled back on the shift leavers to come out of gear. Both shift handles came back, but only one engine came out of gear. We were still in forward gear on one engine and the anchor on the bow was heading for the side window of a commercial fishing boat! I immediately turned off the ignition, but that did nothing to slow down a 12,000 pound boat about to crash through the window of another boat! Dorothy and I ran forward to the bow and managed to push our boat to the side just enough to miss the window.

We got the bow of our boat headed for the dock but

were still moving at a pretty good clip. Dorothy jumped off the boat and onto the dock with the bow rope in her hands. While pulling on the rope to stop the boat, the rope kept slipping through her hands and she got very bad burns. I managed to get on the dock and stop the boat.

After securing the boat, I went down into the engine compartment and discovered that the shifting cable had come loose from the transmission on one engine. It was a simple fix to a problem that nearly caused a disaster.

After one night in Degnen Bay, we exited Gabriola Pass and headed down Tricomali Channel to Conover Cove on Wallace Island. We encountered a strong head wind and choppy seas. In fact, the wind was blowing so hard that it blew our burgee off the bow flag staff and into the water.

As we came into Conover Cove, we saw a small cabin cruiser sitting on the reef in front of the cove. The owners must not have been watching their charts and as they were coming in at high tide, they mistakenly ran over the reef and went aground. Apparently we weren't the only boat that Harold visited. Afterward, we saw a salvage boat heading south along Wallace Island with a damaged boat, flotation bags tied to it and running pumps to keep it afloat.

Something strange happened that evening after dinner when we were relaxing in the main cabin. We heard an odd bumping noise coming from the hull of the boat. Thinking it was a piece of driftwood, I went to push it away. Looking over the side, I was amazed to find a baby seal rubbing against the side of the boat, sucking with its little mouth as it tried to feed itself. I got the boat hook and tried to scare the little guy away because it was sucking on the antifouling paint. I was afraid the paint would harm him. He finally left. A little later we saw the mother seal come back to retrieve her baby. Dorothy and I agreed that the mother seal had been away trying to find food, leaving her baby in the cove for safety.

We'd never been to Prevost Island, so we decided to make it our next stop. We headed south down Trincomali Channel. As we came across the north end of

Navy Channel, we were treated to a great surprise. Looking to the west, I saw a large cluster of boats. At first I thought they were fishing. I got the binoculars and discovered there was a pod of whales close by. They were headed directly for our boat. I shut down the engines and we just sat there drifting. It wasn't long before we had whales all around us. They were swimming on both sides of the boat, even going under the boat and jumping all around us. It was quite thrilling but a little nerve-racking too. We managed to get some great pictures. As the whales headed toward Active Pass, we started the engines and continued toward Prevost Island.

Having decided that none of the bays on the south of Prevost looked inviting enough for overnight anchoring, we went around to the north end and anchored in Annette Inlet. Most of the land around Annette Inlet is private. Therefore we didn't bother to put the dinghy down. Dinner was followed by an early bedtime so we could reach Ganges the next morning.

That night a strong wind came up. As it kept increasing we were concerned about our anchor holding. I got up and turned on the spotlight and discovered we were drifting toward the head of the bay. We'd be aground if we didn't do something. I started the engines and with both of us still in our pajamas, Dorothy took over the helm and began running us out into deeper water. I went to the bow to reset the anchor. We managed to reset the anchor but still weren't getting a good hold. We were drifting back toward the head of the bay, so I put out our second anchor. With both anchors down, we held our ground. The rest of the night we lay in bed listening to the wind howl around the boat. We got up every hour or so to make sure the anchors were still holding.

Suffering from lack of sleep the next day, we headed for Ganges Harbor on Saltspring Island. We took moorage at the government dock at the head of the harbor, then immediately had a nap. We moored the boat with the bow out facing the harbor so it was sitting quite comfortably. With the boat secure at the dock and Dorothy and I a little more rested, we decided to go for a walk to town to buy groceries. On the way, we stopped at a restaurant and made dinner reservations. As we headed back to the boat, it started raining and the evening got chillier. Upon arriving at the boat, I started the diesel heater to warm and dry out the boat.

Then that little black cloud paid us another visit. We were comfortable warming up in the cabin. We'd just finished getting dressed to go to dinner when a wind of steadily increasing velocity started blowing up the harbor. It was hitting the boat directly on the bow. Suddenly, we found the wind was creating a downdraft in the chimney of the diesel heater and causing the flame to go out. This created a lot of heavy black smoke. Before long the whole cabin was filled with the stuff. We shut down the heater and opened all the doors and windows to ventilate the cabin. The cabin eventually cleared, but by then everything in the boat smelled of smoke, ourselves included. We still wanted to go to dinner but all the clothes on board smelled as much as those we had on. We headed for the restaurant anyway. When we got there, we explained what had happened and apologized for smelling like smoke. We were seated in a corner by ourselves beside a window with a beautiful view of the harbor.

The next morning we went to the laundromat and washed the smell out of our clothes.

That afternoon we took in the farmer's market in town before leaving Ganges Harbor. We motored down Swanson Channel and around into Fulford Harbor on the south end of Saltspring Island. We weren't too impressed with the government dock at Fulford Harbor because it was full of old derelict boats that looked like they were about to sink. We decided to stay at the private marina for the night. We walked up the road to the Fulford Inn to look around at the beautiful old building. We bought ice cream cones from the little store at the head of the ferry dock, then went back to the boat to relax for the rest of the day.

The next morning we left Fulford Harbor, deciding to anchor in Princess Margaret Marine Park on Portland Island for the night. Upon arriving at the park, all the buoys were taken. There wasn't enough room to anchor so we moved on down to Sidney Spit Marine Park where we tied to a mooring buoy.

I decided to try my luck at crab fishing. I put the dinghy down, got the crab trap out and headed into deeper water to drop the trap. When I went back to find out how many crabs I'd caught, I found that Harold had paid us another visit. I couldn't find the trap. I discovered I'd set the trap too far out in the channel and the incoming tide with the current had swept it away.

We left Sidney Spit, minus one crab trap, and headed south past James Island. From there, we went past D'Arcy Islands, around Cadboro Point and into Oak Bay. I was about to release the anchor in Oak Bay when I discovered we were right over a sunken boat. Harold would have had a great time with us if our anchor had gotten tangled up in a derelict boat. We moved further out into the bay and set anchor.

The next morning we pulled anchor and headed past the Trail Islands, around Ogden Point breakwater and into Victoria Harbor. There wasn't any room left at the Causeway Floats so we moored at the Wharf Street floats. We stayed in Victoria for three days. In all that time we didn't have a single visit from Harold.

One problem we did have in Victoria harbor was that there was no place to buy propane. Our boat had a propane stove and propane hot water heater and we were running low on fuel. To fill the tank, we had to put the outboard motor on the dinghy, motor all the way through the harbor and under the Johnson Street Bridge, then go to the head of Portage Inlet and carry the tank up the bank to a service station!

After spending three wonderful days in Victoria, we reluctantly left the harbor and headed back up Cordova Channel past James Island. We motored past Swartz Bay and made our way into Satellite Channel with Cowichan Bay as our destination. We were running from the bridge when the clouds began getting heavier and darker. Just as we were pulling into the bay it started raining. We found ourselves in a real downpour. Before we could grab all our belongings and get down to the cabin, everything got soaking wet, including us. We decided this time the little black cloud really did dump on us. We spent a couple of nights in Cowichan Bay with the heater going to dry things out.

From Cowichan Bay, we thought we'd visit Pirates'

Cove on DeCource Island. We traveled through Sansum Narrows and made our way into Stuart Channel. Following Stuart Channel north, we passed on the inside of Kuper and Thetis Islands. We headed for Ruxton Pass between Ruxton and DeCourcy Islands. We then went up the east side of DeCourcy Island and threaded our way past the rock at the entrance to Pirates Cove. Once inside the cove, we set anchor near the dinghy dock.

That's where we met Harold again. It was still early in the afternoon, so we decided to go ashore and walk around the island. The lower end of DeCourcy Island is mostly Marine Park and features some nice trails for easy hiking. After hiking around the Island, we came back to the boat and had dinner. We spent the rest of the evening sitting on the command bridge enjoying the peace and quiet before going to bed. Sometime that night, Harold returned.

I got up early the next morning, made coffee and took it to the back deck to enjoy the morning. I noticed a small oil slick on the water and figured someone was making a big mess in the cove. About that time, I noticed our bilge pump was running and that the oil was coming from our boat. I jumped up, ran into the cabin and immediately turned off the bilge pump. I lifted the engine hatch and looked into the engine area. We had diesel fuel in the bilge!

On further inspection, I discovered the fuel tank on the port side was leaking into the bilge. It was a slow leak and we hadn't spilled much more than a gallon. I put a coffee can under the drip and poured cleaner in the bilge to disperse the diesel oil. When I remodeled the boat I arranged the fuel lines so I could close off one tank and still run both engines from the other tank. Therefore, I proceeded draining the remaining diesel from the port tank to transfer it to the starboard tank. I worked for about thirty minutes but the port tank didn't seem to be getting any lower. I then discovered I had forgotten to close the valve that equalized the fuel between the tanks. Finally, after the port tank was empty we could get under way without spilling diesel fuel in the water.

When we arrived home, I removed the port fuel tank and discovered the nipple between the tank and the shut off valve had cracked. It was about to break off completely. If it had, all the fuel from that tank would have poured into the bilge in less than a half hour!

CHAPTER TWELVE:

North in the Alahanna

In 2003 we took the *Alahanna* north again. On this trip we wanted to get all the way into the Broughton Archipelago. This was one of the most beautiful and enjoyable trips we ever experienced. However, we did find that Harold tagged along also.

One of the places we wanted to visit on our way north was the new marine park on Jedediah Island between Texada Island and Lasqueti Island. We met the *Marizion* in Schooner Cove. The next day, we headed out past the Ballenas Islands, making sure to stay clear of Whisky Gulf and the Canadian Forces test ranges. We then made our way through Bull Passage. We wanted to anchor off Jedediah Island, but there were already too many boats anchored in the bay. Because of the limited space, we moved over to Boho Bay on the Lasqueti Island side.

That afternoon the four of us went aboard our dinghy and crossed over Bull Passage to Jedediah Island. We hiked around the Island, then went down to the far end where we could look out over Bull Island and into the Strait of Georgia. It was getting late and dark clouds were coming in so we decided to head back to the boats before the rain started. When we arrived at the dinghy, the wind came up from a squall blowing through. We jumped into the dinghy and started across Bull Passage. It wasn't raining yet but with the wind blowing down Bull Passage, the sea was getting rough. We didn't get rained on, but we may as well have because the seas were so rough that everyone in the dinghy got soaked from the spray. When we finally arrived back at the boats, we were cold and soaked to the skin. The dinghy ended up with about six inches of water in it. We put on fresh clothes and started the diesel heater to get warm and dry.

From Jedediah Island, we headed north up Okisollo Channel, past Octopus Islands Marine Park, through the Hole in the Wall and into Big Bay on Stuart Island. After negotiating the Yuculta Rapids, the Dent Rapids, the Green Point Rapids in Chancellor Channel and the Whirlpool Rapids in Wellbore Channel, we spent a night in Forward Harbor. We thought we were doing well after negotiating all those rapids, without a visit from Harold. We anchored in Douglas Bay, just inside the entrance to Forward Harbor.

The next day, we decided to go for a walk on the trail going from Douglas Bay, across the peninsula to Bessborough Bay We found it to be a very well marked trail. All along the way people have attached all kinds of items to the bushes and trees. We saw tennis shoes, bleach bottles, old boat bumpers and other debris along the way.

That evening Darrel took the dinghy ashore with their dogs for their evening walk. Suddenly, I looked up and Darrel was rowing the dinghy toward the boats as fast as he could go.

"What's the hurry?" I asked.

Darrel said "I was walking along the beach with the dogs when they both started growling. Then I heard this grunt and the bushes behind me started moving. I decided it was best to get out of there as soon as possible."

We had no idea what was there but we weren't about to go and find out!

Leaving Douglas Bay, we felt sure that Harold would catch up to us as we made our way down Sunderland Channel and back into Johnstone Strait. After entering Johnstone Strait however, we found the wind was light and the seas very calm. We turned into Havannah Channel and along the bottom of East Cracroft Island. We anchored behind Hull Island and waited for slack tide before trying to navigate Chatham Channel. Our destination was Minstrel Island Resort on the south end of Minstrel Island. To get there from Havannah Channel, you must go through Chatham Channel. It's very narrow and you must stay within the marked channel. There are range markers, but we found them to be too far apart. Hence it was very hard to see the next marker after passing the previous one.

We had a friend who grew up in one of the floating camps that moved from island to island during the old days of logging. She'd told us that on weekends loggers and their families came from all the nearby camps to Minstrel Island for the entertainment. In fact that was how the place got its name. They would put on old-fashioned minstrel shows in the lodge!

When we arrived, we were a little disappointed. The resort was quite run down. The fuel dock was closed and we couldn't even get fresh water. We stayed there one night and then went through the Blow Hole into Lagoon Cove Marina on the north end of East Cracroft Island.

Lagoon Cove Marina is a very popular stop. The owners, Bill and Jean Barber, were friendly and accommodating. It was there that we were again visited by Harold. We planned to stay only one night but awoke the next morning to near gale force winds blowing in from the north. However, it turned out to be a good thing. Because of the weather, none of the boats were going to leave. Bill came around to all the boats and announced that we were going to have a happy hour and pot luck in the workshop at the head of the dock.

The guests brought food from their boats, and the marina provided fresh prawns and crab. We were then given a big slice of Jean's home baked bread. After dinner, everybody was invited to the campfire for a marshmallow roast, while Bill told his famous bear stories.

We left Lagoon Cove the next day and found that Harold had visited other boaters as well. We traveled down Knight Inlet for Village Island. Dorothy and I were running a couple miles ahead of the *Marizion* when we passed a small sixteen foot aluminum boat drifting dead in the water. At first we thought it was someone fishing because we saw downriggers coming off both sides of the boat. However, as we passed by we couldn't see anyone in the boat. We were unable to tell if someone had fallen overboard or was lying ill in the bottom. I called Darrel in the *Marazion* on the VHF radio, asking him to stop and take a look as they went by.

As we throttled down to wait, Darrel called back to inform us there was no one in the boat. We turned around and went back to give the *Marazion* a hand. We found the boat had about twelve inches of water in it. All the gear was there but no one was aboard. We started bailing the water out with the intention of taking the boat in tow and calling the Coast Guard.

Suddenly, we saw a large powerboat heading for us at full throttle, blowing it's horn. When the boat got to within calling distance, those aboard yelled at us to leave the boat alone. We discovered they'd been pulling an aluminum fishing boat behind a 45 foot power cruiser. It had broken loose but they didn't discover it missing until they'd traveled several miles down Knight Inlet.

At first they thought we were trying to claim salvage rights until we explained our intentions. They then took the boat back in tow and we all went on our way.

Our next stop was the abandoned Mamalilaculla Indian village on Village Island.

As a teenager living in Oregon, there was a family friend who owned a 42 foot custom built cruiser. The boat was built by Ed Monk Sr. in Seattle in the early 1950s. Every summer he took the boat north. I remember him telling stories of visiting several Indian villages along the way. The natives called him Chief Wrinkle Belly. This was because he was a large, big bellied man who spent all summer sitting at the helm on the command bridge tanning his belly! When he stood up there were white streaks accenting the wrinkles.

One summer their boat had engine troubles. The problem was discovered to be a broken crankshaft. The nearest stopping place was one of these Indian villages. The natives helped remove the engine and disassembled it on the dock. They called home on the ship-to-shore radio and had a new crankshaft flown in by float plane. It took over a week to get the engine repaired and back into the boat. The skipper and his crew became good friends with the local people during that time and he came home with a genuine native dug-out canoe in tow as a gift. I'm not sure but I think this took place on Village Island. That's why we wanted to make this island one of our stops.

We spent a night at the dock on Village Island. The village had been abandoned for several years and all of the buildings had fallen into decay. We could see where the Long House once stood and the building that probably served as the hospital was still standing. There were also a few rotting totem poles lying on the ground covered with blackberry vines.

From Village Island we made our way down Village Channel, past the bottom of Crease Island and Swanson Island, and out into Blackfish Sound. We fished Blackfish Sound for a few hours and caught an eighteen pound salmon. Then, hoping to see some whales, we left and headed for Robson Bight in Johnstone Strait. We drifted around the Bight for a couple hours and saw whales far off at the mouth of the Tsitika River. The area is a gathering place and summer breeding area for the northern killer whales. Because of this, it's a protected area and boaters are required to stay at least one half mile off shore, so we couldn't get close enough for a good view.

We left Robson Bight and went into Telegraph Cove. We spent one night in Telegraph Cove with the intention of leaving the next morning to go to Alert Bay. Then Harold came back. We awoke the next morning and found ourselves fogged in. The following morning the fog lifted and we were able to get over to Alert Bay on Cormorant Island. Several attractions in Alert Bay are a must-see. The U'Mista Cultural Center, the Gater Gardens, the Namgis burial grounds, the old Anglican church, the old residential school and the world's tallest totem pole to list a few. We stayed three days there and were able to take it all in. Because we spent so much time in Alert Bay, our vacation time was running short. As bad as we wanted to continue on into the Broughton Archipelago, we had to head home.

On our way home, our first overnight stop was Lagoon Cove again. We looked at the chart and found we could get back there through Beware Passage or Baronet Passage by going through Clio Channel and on into Lagoon Cove. We looked closely at Beware Passage with all the rocks and narrow passes, and decided it would be an open invitation to Harold. Baronet Passage seemed a better choice.

We followed the same route home we'd taken going up. The only exception was that, when going down Calm Channel from Stuart Island, we turned and went into Pryce Channel instead of going through the Hole in the Wall. We came across the north end of West Redonda Island and down through Waddington Channel, then anchored for a night in Walsh Cove Marine Park before going into Desolation Sound Marine Park. From there we navigated past the Copeland Islands and into Lund for fuel and an overnight stop. The next day, we passed Powell River and into Malaspina Strait. We made an overnight stop in Pender Harbor and then headed home.

CHAPTER THIRTEEN:

Harold Goes to Lower Puget Sound

In the summer of 2000, we took the *Alahanna* on a cruise to the lower Puget Sound in Washington State. Harold came along but we managed to avoid him for most of the trip.

We left Reed Point Marina on a clear, sunny August morning. We navigated through the Second Narrows, then under the First Narrows Bridge. The *Alahanna* has a cruising speed of nine and one half knots, running her twin diesel engines at 1900 R.P.M. At full throttle her top speed is just under fourteen knots. With that kind of speed, we could negotiate almost any narrows or pass regardless of the tide currents.

After going through the First Narrows, we set a course for Silva Bay on Gabriola Island. We had perfect sea conditions crossing the Strait of Georgia so we arrived in Silva Bay around lunch time. Entering Silva Bay from the Flat Top Islands and going through Commodore Passage, we made our way between Tugboat and Vance Islands. It's important to watch the channel markers and give the beacon that marks Shipyard Rock a wide birth to the port. It's easy to miss that marker and head straight for Silva Bay.

As we were entered the bay, we saw where Harold had visited a sailboat which had come through the pass at about mid tide. It's crew hadn't seen the beacon and had run aground on Shipyard Rock. After setting our anchor, we had lunch aboard. By mid afternoon the bay got crowded. We decided to pull anchor and go through Gabriola Pass, where we spent the night in Degnen Bay.

The next morning, we worked our way down Trincomali Channel, on through Swanson Channel and into Sidney Spit Marine Park. Once there we took a mooring buoy for the night. After spending one night in Sidney Spit, we went across to Port Sidney and cleared customs in preparation to leave Canada. We then traveled across Haro Strait and entered U. S. waters. After you have cleared U. S. customs for the first time, they give you a registration number. With this number, we could phone customs and get clearance without going into their ports. As we approached Stewart Island, we phoned and received a clearance number. We then headed for Reid Harbor and tied to a mooring buoy for the night. The next day we made our way to Friday Harbor on San Juan Island where we stopped for fuel and supplies. From Friday Harbor, we decided to go into Fisherman's Bay on Lopez Island and take moorage for the night.

It was while on Lopez Island that Harold nearly got us. The entrance into Fisherman Bay is narrow and shallow. We had to avoid a drying shoal about 200 yards off the entrance. Going through the entrance with larger boats on anything less then half tide isn't recommended. We made our way through the entrance at close to high tide with no problem. After dinner we consulted our tide book and set a time to leave in the morning. We didn't want to attempt going out the entrance in anything less than mid-tide.

The next morning I awoke, looked at my watch, and discovered we'd slept in by nearly an hour. We quickly had breakfast, untied the mooring lines and headed for the entrance. We decided to run the boat from the command bridge because we had better visibility from there.

As we started through the channel, the depth sounder was showing five feet of water under us. The *Alahanna* needs about three and one half feet under her keel to keep afloat. We decided to go ahead and give it a try. Looking over the side, I could see the bottom but thought we still had a couple feet extra under us. About half way through the channel, I looked behind the boat and saw we were stirring up a lot of mud. I knew the propellers weren't hitting bottom yet so we kept going. We finally made it into deeper water without touching bottom! We then thanked Harold for not coming aboard.

From Fisherman Bay, our next stop was Spencer Spit on the northeast corner of Lopez Island. We anchored in the little bay south of the spit and put the dinghy down and went ashore to do some exploring.

The next morning, we awakened to fog, a light rain and limited visibility. We wondered if this was more of Harold's doing. Our plan was to head towards Anacortes and go through Swinomish Channel into LaConner.

A couple years previously, I'd purchased a navigation program for my laptop computer. The program interfaced with our onboard GPS, tracking the boat on the chart shown on the computer screen. As we made our way through Thatcher Pass and started across Rosario Strait, we were glad we had this navigation aid on board. Even though it's a good way to navigate, Dorothy always had the paper charts spread out on the table in front of her.

She said, "I like to see where I'm going on the chart rather than have to depend on some electronic device."

Just as we started into Padilla Bay, Harold showed up. Suddenly, I wasn't getting a reading from the GPS. I had the chart on the computer but it wasn't showing the boat. I turned to Dorothy and her paper chart. We set a compass course in the fog for the entrance to Swinomish Channel. Luckily we found the channel and, once inside, the navigating was much easier.

By this time the rain had stopped. The fog lifted, and the sun was coming out. We traveled down the channel admiring all the beautiful waterfront homes with their perfectly landscaped yards. As we approached the

LaConner waterfront, we had the current going with us. I knew from my boating experience on the Columbia River that it was best to travel past the spot on the dock you wanted, then turn around and approach coming back against the current. I followed this procedure and made a perfect landing. We watched a couple of other boats approach the dock by going in with the current. They missed their spot by several boat lengths.

I spent most of the remainder of the day trying to find the problem with the navigation program. We knew that the next day we'd be going through Skagit Bay, which is very large and shallow. At mid tide or higher we couldn't see the channel. It was important to follow the channel or we could run aground, so I wanted the computer working for this leg of the trip. Just before dinner, I found a corroded connection between the laptop and the GPS. After cleaning the contacts, everything was working again.

While we were sitting aboard the boat in LaConner, an older couple came down and went aboard a boat that was around 45 feet long. We watched while they performed one of the best examples of seamanship we'd ever seen. They both had two-way radios clipped to their belts with small headphones on with microphones attached. He got in the boat and started the engines while she went forward to untie the bow line.

They sat at the dock with the current running against

their stern. To get out of their spot, it was necessary to move the boat back against the current, away from the dock and then forward to leave, missing the boat moored ahead of them. We saw their mouths moving as they quietly talked to each other, letting one another know what they were doing. As she untied the bow, he put the boat in reverse to hold it against the current. She then walked down the side of the boat, untied the stern and stepped aboard. Using his twin engines he slowly walked the bow away from the dock, followed by the stern and off they went. We were amazed by how they accomplished this so smoothly, without any yelling back and forth.

Our next stop was the town of Langley on Whidbey Island. We came out of Skaget Bay and into Saratoga Passage. The rain returned so we ran the boat from the lower station. I had a small three blade defroster fan mounted on the dash to keep the window from fogging over. Suddenly, one blade of the fan broke off and went flying across the cabin, just missing us. "Thanks Harold", we said. Dorothy handed me a towel to keep the window clear.

We decided to skip Langley and head for the Port of Everett where we could buy a new fan at the marine supply store. We were told that the Port of Everett is the largest private marina north of Marina Del Ray in California. It's also the U.S. naval base for the Puget Sound area. Their visitors' dock is on one of the outside floats. After getting assigned a spot, we pulled into the dock and tied up. We then had to walk almost a quarter mile just to get to the shore and then, several more blocks to the store. While looking at the different types of fans that were available, and cringing at the prices, I looked down and in a bin below were fan blades only. They were about one third of the price of a new fan. We bought a blade and headed back to the boat to replace the fan blade.

We were told by several friends that when in the Seattle area, a must-see is Blake Island. After leaving the Port of Everett, we decided to make it our next stop.

Blake Island is a Washington State Marine Park. It's located across Puget Sound from Seattle's Elliott Bay. Upon our arrival, we found there wasn't any dock space available. We were told we could poll tie inside the breakwater and come to shore by dinghy. We didn't know what was meant by poll tying but after seeing other boats over there, we decided to follow their example. There are pilings just inside the breakwater in rows spaced about fifty feet apart. We positioned the boat between two pilings. We then attached a line to the bow cleat, ran it through the chock on the port side, around the piling and back through the chock on the starboard side. At the stern we did the same, tied a line from the port cleat, around the piling and back to the starboard cleat. We left enough slack on both lines that allowed the boat to ride up and down on the piling with the tide. We stayed tied this way for two days and two nights, with no problems.

The main attraction on Blake Island is the replica of a native long house built by the Tillicum Indian Band. In the evenings they put on a barbeque salmon dinner followed by a live stage show. We decided to attend. The dinner started with a bowel of butter clams that you ate outside. After eating the clams, the shells are tossed on the ground. The whole area was covered with crushed shells. We devoured the clam appetizers, and were ushered into a long house where we were served our fresh salmon dinner that had been cooked over an open fire. After dinner, the show started. It was a live stage show depicting the life history of the Tillicum Indians, complete with authentic native dances.

From Blake Island, we went to Gig Harbor where we shopped for food and supplies. After a night in Gig Harbor, we traveled through Tacoma Narrows, up Hale Passage on the north side of Fox Island and into Carr Inlet. We went into Penrose Point State Park at Mayo Cove and tied to a mooring buoy, then lowered the dinghy to go ashore for some exploring. While ashore, we talked to some local boaters. They were surprised to hear that we'd just come through the Tacoma Narrows.

"We wouldn't attempt to negotiate those narrows when the current is running as strong as it must have been when you came through," they said.

"Compared to some of the passes we have in the

Canadian waters, the Tacoma Narrows is nothing," we replied.

We'd made arrangements to pick up Dorothy's brother and sister-in-law in Steilacoom and have them come aboard for a few days. We headed for Steilacoom, looking for the local marina. After getting our guests aboard, we headed through Balch Passage and anchored in Filucy Bay. We put the dinghy down and went over to Longbranch Marina for some exploring.

Our next stop was Olympia, the capitol of Washington State. We navigated through Dana Passage and down Budd Inlet. We took moorage at Percival Landing Park at the head of Budd Inlet. So far we'd avoided Harold. We spent a couple days in Olympia, exploring the stores and walking up to the capitol buildings.

From Olympia, we went back to Steilacoom, where we dropped off Dorothy's brother and sister-in-law. We then headed up Case Inlet, down Pickering Passage and into Jarrell Cove on the North end of Harstine Island. We anchored across from the Marina next to Jerrell Cove Marine State Park. This is where Harold came for a visit. We'd just put the dinghy in the water and were getting ready to go ashore when the sky opened up. A hard rain started. We were soaked before we could secure the dinghy. We sat in the cabin and watched the rain for almost a half hour. Then the sun came out and once again it was warm, the skies clear.

The next day, we took a side trip up Case Inlet and anchored off Stretch Island at Stretch Point Marine State Park. While there, we went ashore and dug some butter clams to make clam chowder. We also took the dinghy over to Fair Harbor and looked around the Marina. Not wanting to encourage another visit from Harold, we decided that Stretch Point was too open and exposed if a wind should come up, so we went back to Jerroll Cove for the night.

The next morning, we headed north through Tacoma Narrows and made our way into Quartermaster Harbor on Vashon Island. We wanted to stop and visit the village of Burton, but upon arrival, we found the Marina was full. We then went back to Dockton Park on the west side of Maury Island and took moorage at one of their guest slips.

By then, three weeks into our holidays, we decided to start heading for home. We needed fuel and supplies so we made a stop in Seattle. After traveling north up Puget Sound, we turned into Elliott Bay and stopped at Bell Harbor Marina. Bell Harbor is one of Seattle's newest full service marinas and is run by the Port of Seattle. Located in the heart of downtown Seattle, it's only a short walk away from the famous Pike Place Market.

There's a trolley that runs the length of the waterfront and goes all the way to Pioneer Square. We left the boat at Bell Harbor Marina and took the trolley up the waterfront to Iver's seafood restaurant. There, we enjoyed a great clam chowder dinner. After dinner, we walked back to the boat along the waterfront, stopping at a few of the shops on the way. We had a good night's sleep aboard.

The next morning, we left Seattle and headed for Canadian waters. As we made our way up Saratoga Passage, we thought we'd try once more to get a slip at the Langley Boat Harbor on Whidbey Island. This time we actually found a spot, so we decided to stay for at least one day. Our visit to the little town of Langley turned out to be very worthwhile. The main street is lined with restored buildings that house many interesting shops and eateries. We even found a great bakery where we had lunch.

We wanted to explore Holmes Harbor and Camano Island State Park as well as the town of Coupeville in Penn Cove. However, time was running short. So far, we'd managed to avoid any visits from Harold, so we headed straight for La Conner where we stayed for one night. The next night, we were in Fossel Bay on Sucia Island. We crossed Haro Strait and went into the public dock in Bedwell Harbor on South Pender Island, where we cleared customs. We then navigated through the Pender canal and took moorage at Port Browning Marina for the night.

We made our way up through the Gulf Islands. The remainder of out trip was uneventful until we started through Dodd Narrows. It was then that our good fortune was interrupted by Harold. We decided we'd spend a couple nights anchored in Newcastle Island Marine Park, across from Nanaimo. Following that, we'd cross the Strait of Georgia and go home.

It was a sunny day with little wind. The seas were calm as we made our way up Stuart Channel. We approached Dodd Narrows at about one hour past slack tide. We were running against an ebb tide of around four knots. That wasn't difficult to handle with the *Alahanna's* speed. We sat at the south end of the narrows listening to the radio as south-bound boats announced their passage. Finally, when all was clear, we radioed our passage and headed north. We looked to our stern and saw there were three other boats going through with us.

We'd just broken out into Northumberland Channel when the starboard engine suddenly quit. That cut our speed down by more than half. I looked aft and the other boats were rapidly gaining on us. I managed to pull over to the east side of the channel and give the other boats room to pass. I gave the port engine full throttle and put Dorothy at the helm. This gave us enough speed to make a little headway. I went down into the engine room and quickly discovered the starboard engine wasn't getting fuel. The problem turned out to be a plugged fuel filter. Using one of the spare fuel filters I always carry aboard, I replaced the filter and the engine started immediately.

We took anchorage in Newcastle Island Marine Park, put the dinghy down and motored over to Nanaimo Public Dock. We walked up to the local marine supply store and bought a new replacement fuel filter. After spending a couple nights in Newcastle, we headed across the Strait of Georgia and made our way home.

We did two long cruises in the *Alahanna.* The first one was our trip to the Broughton Archipelago discussed in the previous chapter, then this trip to the lower Puget Sound.

The total distance covered on the first trip was 450 nautical miles. We used 216 gallons of fuel and spent 60 hours at the helm. The total distance covered on our Puget Sound cruise was a little over 600 nautical miles. We burned 278 gallons of diesel and were at the helm for just under 80 hours.

CHAPTER FOURTEEN:

A Visit from Angels

Most of Harold's visits seemed insignificant, but a couple of times, it was a wonder we survived at all. One was when we were anchored in Montague Harbor on Galiano Island. Our granddaughter was visiting her grandparents, who lived on Galliano Island and we invited her to stay aboard our boat for the night.

The next afternoon, we took her ashore. We were preparing to leave the harbor with the intention of meeting the *Marazion* in Ganges on Salt Spring Island. The good weather began deteriorating and we could hear thunder in the distance. I opened the hatch to the lazaret on the back deck and prepared to remove the outboard motor from the dinghy to store it below. From there I could load the dinghy onto the swim grid. We'd pull anchor and be on our way, or so I thought. Harold had a different plan for us. About that time there was a loud clap of thunder. Dorothy came running out of the cabin and fell through the open hatch!

I was in the dinghy and had my back to the boat when I heard a loud crash. I turned around to see what all the noise was about and there was Dorothy sitting on the back deck with her legs down in the lazaret. She had this strange look on her face and said,

“I think I just broke my leg”.

As I looked back into the boat, she lifted her right leg up, and her foot was pointing straight down. I grabbed some light rope and made a splint to put on her leg to help hold her foot in place. I managed to get her into the dinghy and we made our way to the marina. The marina owners were very accommodating and brought us a jacket and some blankets to keep Dorothy warm so she wouldn’t go into shock.

We then phoned the ambulance on Galliano Island. Soon the paramedics showed up to have a look. The whole time, Dorothy lay in the dinghy and claimed to not be in too much pain. Maybe that was because, before leaving the boat, she’d taken a couple Tylenol 222 pain killers left over from dental work she’d had done. The paramedics put a temporary splint and soft cast on her leg and concluded that she needed to be sent to the hospital on Salt Spring Island. They called for the water ambulance from Ganges to come over and transport her.

Just as we were heading out of Montague Harbor, I heard the *Marazion* calling us on the radio. The skipper allowed me to answer them and I explained that we’d had another visit from Harold. At that time we thought we’d take Dorothy to the hospital on Salt Spring, have a cast put on her, and she’d be sent home. We were still hoping to meet the *Marazion* in Ganges. Then the paramedics informed us that the break was too serious to be taken care of in the Salt Spring hospital. They called for another ambulance to meet us in Swartz Bay to take Dorothy to the Sannich hospital where they had the proper facilities to take care of the fracture. We called the *Marazion* back, telling them to go on and that we'd call them after all this was settled.

In the mean time the paramedics kept asking Dorothy,

"On a scale of one to ten how bad is the pain?"

It was probably the Tylenol talking when she said,

"Oh, only about a four or five."

We were put into an ambulance at Swartz Bay and taken to the hospital in Sannich. We waited for over an hour with Dorothy laying on a gurney in the hallway next to the cardiac arrest room. Finally they took her in to x-ray her leg. Then we waited for another 45 minutes before seeing a doctor. When the doctor arrived and showed us the x-rays, he explained that it wasn't a clean break. She had splintered her tibia, cracked her fibula, and broken her ankle.

Upon analyzing the fall, we concluded that when she fell into the lazaret, her left leg and body fell in while her right foot was on the non-skid deck. As her body twisted, her right foot couldn't twist with it because of the non-skid on the deck. Hence, instead of a nice clean break, she had a very bad splinter type break. Then we received the really bad news. The doctor said this was going to require some very serious surgery and he wouldn't operate if he couldn't do the follow-up. He said he didn't think we wanted to stay around Saanich for the next couple of months. The staff at the Saanich hospital then called Royal Columbian hospital in New Westminster. An available bed was found and the operation would be preformed there.

An ambulance was called again to pick us up and take us on the ferry from Swartz Bay to Tsawwassen. When we arrived at Tsawwassen, we found there was another ambulance waiting for us. Once more we were transferred because the Saanich ambulance had to go back to the Island. We finally arrived at Royal Columbian hospital around 7:00 pm. Hence, we were in New Westminster without transportation. The boat was left sitting at anchor in Montague Harbor with the dinghy at the marina. I phoned the marina and they assured us that the dinghy would be looked after and they'd keep an eye on our boat.

Upon arriving at Royal Columbian hospital, the staff told us the doctor who would do the surgery had gone home. They asked us if we had eaten anything. We said not since breakfast, so they brought us sandwiches and a drink. We'd just finished the sandwiches when along came the surgeon to have a look at Dorothy's leg. He hadn't gone home after all, but decided that as long as he was still there, he might as well do the operation. He then asked Dorothy when she'd last eaten. When she told him she'd just had a sandwich and a drink, the operation was called off.

The operation was performed the following morning. After five days in the hospital, Dorothy was sent home with a steel plate in her leg, a pin in her ankle, and a row of staples down the front of her leg. She spent the next two months in a wheelchair and on crutches.

Dorothy's broken leg was the start of a completely new learning experience for us. Learning how to use crutches was harder than it looked, especially going up and down stairs. Being in a wheelchair wasn't very convenient when shopping either. We found the two major shopping malls in our area at that time didn't have elevators for wheelchair shoppers to access the upper level. In both malls, the only way to get to the upper level was to use the freight elevator in the Hudson's Bay store. While shopping for lady's clothing in one department store, we discovered that the racks were positioned so close together that we couldn't get the wheelchair between them.

Dorothy had to keep her leg elevated whenever possible. We installed a leg support on the wheelchair. While grocery shopping at the supermarket, I would walk behind her pulling the grocery cart. Because of Dorothy's protruding broken leg, whenever we came to the end of an isle, I'd check to see that our way was clear

One morning, because of an early morning meeting, I

got myself into big trouble. Dorothy said she'd be fine getting up on her own. I got up, said goodbye and left the house. Not thinking, I set the alarm as I went out the door. Our bedroom is up four steps above the main part of the house. Dorothy got up, retrieved her crutches, left the bedroom and started down the stairs into the hallway. This activated the motion detector which set off the alarm and started the horn to sound. Dorothy was struggling to get down and turn off the alarm when the phone started ringing. After eventually getting the alarm turned off, she answered the phone. It was, of course, the alarm company calling. By then, everything was okay with them but I was in real trouble. I still get blamed, not only for breaking her leg the first time on our boat, but for also trying a second time when the alarm was activated.

Subsequent trouble came from Harold a couple of years later when Dorothy and I were in the middle of the Strait of Georgia, halfway between Silva Bay and Gibsons on the Sunshine Coast. We'd spent the night anchored in Silva Bay and planned to leave in the morning. We'd then stay one night at the public dock in Gibsons before heading home. A strong wind blew all night and into the following morning when we got up. After breakfast, we decided to see if the wind would calm down enough for us to make the crossing.

Around noon, the wind began lessened so we had lunch and waited another hour. As the weather began looking better, we decided to pull anchor and have a look. Once out of Silva Bay and into the Strait, it didn't look too bad, so we headed across. The seas had calmed somewhat, the waves were only about two feet high. A northwest wind was blowing at about twelve knots. Unfortunately, as we made our way across, the wind increased again and the seas grew rougher. We were now a little over half way across. The waves were increasing to five or six feet in height. We were taking them off our port bow but were still able to keep the boat under control. We reasoned that if we turned around at that time, it would be of no advantage, so we kept heading toward Gibsons.

The seas grew more turbulent, but we stayed our course. Dorothy and I were both on the bridge. I could see better from up there to keep the boat heading into the waves. As we came off the crest of a wave and headed into the trough, the boat would bury the bow into the next wave. I tried to keep the bow heading into the on-coming wave. That kept the boat from turning sideways in between waves and putting us into a rollover situation.

We were doing fine and holding our own for a while. Then we came down the backside of a wave and, as I turned the wheel, nothing happened. The boat fell into the trough between waves and went into a heavy roll that nearly threw Dorothy and me off the bridge. I knew immediately that we'd broken another hydraulic steering line. I managed to make my way off the bridge and down into the cabin. However, the boat was pitching from side to side so badly that I could hardly stand up. I was being tossed from one side of the cabin to the other and couldn't get the engine hatch open to access the engine room.

I went back up on the bridge and had the radio microphone in my hand. I was about to put in a mayday call to the Coast Guard. Suddenly Dorothy looked up and said, "Look, there's a boat coming toward us". I could see a 26 foot Bayliner heading straight for us. It was not more than a quarter of a mile away. As it approached we could see two men aboard. They came alongside, as close as the sea conditions would allow. They asked if we could use some help. I told them that if they could take us in tow and just hold our bow into the waves, I could get into the engine room and repair the broken line. I had a spare 100 foot line aboard so I grabbed it and made my way up onto the bow. After securing the line onto our bow cleat and throwing the other end to the Bayliner, they took us in tow and held our bow into the waves so we were not being pitched from side to side. That way, I could get the hatch open to the engine room and find the break. It took only a short time to repair the break in the line.

I then went back onto the bridge and put some more hydraulic fluid into the system and we had steering back. I made my way up onto the bow and signaled to the Bayliner that all was repaired and we could be turned loose. I asked one of the men for his name and address so I could pay them for their help. He said his name was Bruce and not to worry about it. I headed back to the bridge and when I turned to give them a wave goodbye, they were nowhere in sight.

We are Christians and we have always had faith in the Lord. We also believe we all have a guardian angel looking over us. This was the first time we'd had the opportunity to be pulled out of a bad situation by someone we were sure was our guardian angel. After thinking about it, we realized we hadn't seen a name on the transom or a registration number on the bow. Also, their boat was smaller than ours. They shouldn't have been out there in that kind of weather either. Bruce and his friend seemed to have suddenly appeared out of nowhere and disappeared without a trace. Once they'd departed the seas started to calm down. We had a much more comfortable ride on into Gibsons. Whether this was our guardian angel or not is debatable but we like to believe he was. Our guardian angel's name is Bruce.

Upon arriving at the public dock in Gibsons, Dorothy and I sat in the boat thinking about what had just happened. We realized how bad the situation had been. Thinking back, we couldn't describe what Bruce and his friend looked like. This was one of the worst situations Harold had ever put us in. Even if we had contacted the Coast Guard, they probably wouldn't have made it in time. We then said a prayer, thanking God for sending Bruce to save us.

Later on I found that the hydraulic lines I had used to install the steering system were the wrong type of line. I'd used a soft wall line and therefore the heat from the engines caused the line to give way. I replaced all the hydraulic lines with the proper hard walled line and everything then seemed good. No more broken steering.

The experiences I've related took place over a span of more than sixty years. I've opted to share them here, in part, because there's no shortage of books about nice cruising times. Those of you who've faced adversities on the water may find this account encouraging, perhaps even getting a good laugh from some of what I've written. It is hoped that we've learned from our mistakes and the unexpected mishaps. It is further hoped that we are better boaters and better people as a result of what we've been through. The difficulties we encountered can either be ascribed to our own negligence at times or that mysterious little black cloud Harold. Either way, we're persuaded that those hardships have taught us some valuable life lessons.

We sold the *Alahanna* and now own a diesel powered pickup and a 28-foot fifth wheel. We are enjoying land cruising. I think the proper term is RVing. It's not that different from boating but instead of going into a marina we go to an R.V. park. Instead of a nice little bay, we head for a forestry camp. And yes, Harold still pays us a visit in the fifth wheel every once in a while, and we're still learning from him.

Les and Dorothy

With the Alahanna

GLOSSARY

BUCKTAIL FISHING – Fishing for salmon using a feathered hook pulled by a boat floating near the surface.

BURGEE – A small flag displayed by boats for identification.

CHOCK – A metal fitting with two inward curved jaws through which a rope can be run.

CLEAT – A metal fitting with projecting ends on which a rope can be secured.

DOWNRIGGER – A device attached to a boat used to lower and raise fishing gear to a desired depth.

EBB TIDE – The outgoing tide.

FLOOD TIDE – The incoming tide.

GUNNELS – The upper edge of a boats side.

HELM – The steering station of a boat.

LAZERET – The storage space below the rear deck of a boat.

LOG RACE – A boat race where the captain

predetermines how long it will take to travel from one point to another at a certain speed.

OUTDRIVE – The drive mechanism located outside on the back of a boat.

RAFTED – Two or more boats tied side by side.

RISER – The part of a marine engine where the exhaust mixes with the cooling water before exiting overboard.

Made in the USA
Charleston, SC
04 November 2015